FINANCIAL TIMES
MANAGEMENT

Knowledge   Skills   Understanding

Financial Times Management is a new business created to deliver the knowledge, skills and understanding that will enable students, managers and organisations to achieve their ambitions, whatever their needs, wherever they are.

To find out more about Financial Times Management visit our website at:

www.ftmanagement.com

Financial Times Management Briefings are happy to receive proposals from individuals who have expertise in the field of management education.

If you would like to discuss your ideas further, please contact Andrew Mould, Commissioning Editor.

Tel: 0171 447 2210
Fax: 0171 240 5771
e-mail: andrew.mould@ftmanagement.com

MANAGEMENT BRIEFINGS

Financial Performance Measurement and Shareholder Value Explained

ALAN WARNER

AND

ALISON HENNELL

FINANCIAL TIMES
MANAGEMENT

LONDON · HONG KONG · JOHANNESBURG
MELBOURNE · SINGAPORE · WASHINGTON DC

FINANCIAL TIMES MANAGEMENT
128 Long Acre, London WC2E 9AN
Tel: +44 (0)171 447 2000
Fax: +44 (0)171 240 5771
Website: www.ftmanagement.com

A Division of Financial Times Professional Limited

First published in Great Britain in 1998

ISBN 0 273 63576 X

British Library Cataloguing in Publication Data
A CIP catalogue record for this book can be obtained from the British Library.

10 9 8 7 6 5 4 3 2 1

Printed and bound in Great Britain.

The Publishers' policy is to use paper manufactured from sustainable forests.

About the authors

Alan Warner is a qualified chartered management accountant, formerly Director of Studies at Ashridge Management College and a founding member of the Management Training Partnership (MTP). He has written a wide range of articles on financial, management and HR issues appearing in *The Times, Management Today, Personnel Management* and all the major accounting journals. In recent years his writing efforts have been concentrated on a unique trilogy of books which are all in the form of novels which make difficult topics easy to understand and apply.

Alison Hennell is a chartered accountant having qualified with Coopers & Lybrand, and is also a member of the Management Training Partnership. She moved into management training when she joined MTP in 1995.

The Management Training Partnership was formed in 1987 by three senior staff at Ashridge Management College and has rapidly grown to become one of the largest UK providers of tailored management training.

MTP designs and delivers tailored programmes in three core topic areas: Finance, Marketing/Strategy and Behavioural Skills. The Partnership has a range of blue-chip clients including Unilever, British Airways, BP and Boots, and employs 15 full-time tutors, all specialists with management experience.

For further information please contact:

Alan Warner
Management Training Partnership plc
3 Prebendal Court
Oxford Road
AYLESBURY
Bucks
HP19 3EY

Tel: 01296 423474
Fax: 01296 393879
e-mail: mtp_alanwarner@compuserve.com

CONTENTS

PREFACE

This book sets out to explain the concept of shareholder value, how it is measured and the ways in which it can be maximised within a business.

It is theoretically rigorous but cuts through the jargon and formulae usually associated with this subject. The end result is an independent review of the different value creation models together with practical advice on how such a system should be implemented.

The starting point of the book is a review of the need for performance measures and the introduction of the concept of shareholder value. Conventional financial measures are then discussed together with their inherent limitations.

Later chapters review the new metrics being used by companies, shareholders and analysts to measure value creation. The publication finishes with some practical advice on implementing shareholder value measures throughout a business.

The book is suitable for use on any course that addresses the concept of shareholder value. Its practical nature demonstrates the skills and ability of the Management Training Partnership to provide user-friendly and effective learning for all managers.

LIST OF ABBREVIATIONS

BCG	Boston Consulting Group
CAPM	capital asset pricing model
CE	chief executive
CEO	chief executive officer
CFO	chief financial officer
CFROI	cash flow return on investment
CVA	customer value added
DCF	discounted cash flow
EBIT	earnings before interest and tax
EPS	earnings per share
EVA	economic value added
FMCG	fast moving consumer goods
FTSE 100	Financial Times Stock Exchange 100-Share Index
IRR	internal rate of return
KPI	key performance indicator
MVA	market value added
NOPAT	net operating profit after tax
NPV	net present value
OCF	operating cash flow
P/E	price/earnings ratio
PVA	people value added
R&D	research and development
ROC	return on capital
ROCE	return on capital employed
ROE	return on equity
ROI	return on investment
RONA	return on net assets
ROS	return on sales

TBR	total business return
TSR	total shareholder return
VBM	value-based management
WACC	weighted average cost of capital
WYMIWYG	'what you measure is what you get'
WYRIWYG	'what you reward is what you get'

1

The broader context of financial performance measurement

> 'Management don't get paid to make shareholders comfortable, it gets paid to make them rich.'
>
> Robert Goizueta, CEO Coca-Cola (1981–98)

WYMIWYG – WHAT YOU MEASURE IS WHAT YOU GET!

Financial performance measurement is a topic which should consume the attention of managers at all levels and in all functions of the modern business. It is far too important to be left to the accountants because it is much more than a financial issue.

Performance measures are a key factor in driving management behaviour which means that all managers should understand the concepts behind them and have a say in their development. Financial measures only achieve their objectives if managers understand and are motivated by them.

WYMIWYG – 'what you measure is what you get' – is an acronym which should be remembered throughout this book. It is a reminder of the impact of performance measures on management behaviour which can be both positive and negative. There is something about the make-up of competitive and ambitious managers – the sort employed by top companies – that drives them to find ways which maximise performance of their department or division. This can often be at the expense of the business as a whole and may even fly in the face of common sense.

If arguing about the transfer price or the cost allocation system is the action most likely to maximise profits, that is what they will do, even if they know in their hearts that it is not a value-adding activity. Top management will be wasting their time asking their divisional managers to focus on cash flow if the key performance measure is operating profit. And if the performance measures go through to the pay packets of the managers involved by means of some kind of bonus, WYMIWYG is even more likely to apply.

THE IMPLICATIONS OF WYMIWYG FOR SHAREHOLDER VALUE MEASUREMENT

Despite what may seem its obvious nature, the WYMIWYG principle has not until recently had as big an impact on management thinking as it should. It therefore came as something of a surprise to some management analysts that the move of companies like Coca-Cola and Quaker to a performance system based on 'shareholder value' should have such an apparently direct and positive impact. Share prices went up merely on the announcement of such a move.

Articles such as the one in *Fortune* magazine in September 1993, showing correlations between moves to shareholder value measures and share price, only served to increase the likelihood of further correlations. It must say something about the concern in the financial community about existing practice that a mere announcement can have such an impact. One cynical investor relations manager of a high-profile FTSE 100 company told us that mentioning a change to shareholder value measures was essential at analysts' meetings and you could see all the analysts ticking it off their lists. It was reported in *Antidote* magazine in 1996 that the number of times the term 'shareholder value' was mentioned in *The Financial Times* had increased from under 100 in 1993 to nearly 400 in 1996.

This reaction from the stock market raises a key question. Can the top management of these companies really have been so lacking that they had not previously aligned the key performance measures within their businesses to the success criteria which their employers, the shareholders, regarded as important? The answer is yes but this is not quite so negligent as it may seem. As this book will demonstrate, it is not that easy to determine what is meant by shareholder value and it is even more difficult to create a perfect alignment with measures which operational managers can drive. Before we begin to explore this alignment, we will first have a look at a definition of shareholder value. How is this value created?

THE CREATION OF SHAREHOLDER VALUE

Most measures of operational performance derive from accounting concepts, in particular from definitions of cost and profit which depend on generally accepted accounting principles. Though there is clearly some link between profit and shareholder value, the content of this book will show that shareholder value is not driven by profit alone. Shareholders do not judge company performance solely by profit measures and this trend is increasing.

For a publicly quoted company, the best way to see shareholder value is to think of yourself and other individuals who buy shares on the stock market. What pay-off are they looking for? How do they measure the success of their investments? Most individuals invest in the stock market to achieve some sort of capital gain and it is therefore the growth in market price after purchase which is the focus of their attention. Profit may be one of the drivers of this growth in market price but it will not be the only one. Share prices tend to reflect expectations of future prospects as well as past or present performance.

When it comes to evaluating the success of a particular investment in shares – the value which has been created for that shareholder – the obvious calculation would be the difference between what was originally paid and what the share was later sold for. That is real value for the shareholders and it is a key factor in how analysts in the world's stock exchanges assess the relative performance of the shares they deal in. It is also how they assess the performance of the top management running those companies.

There is, however, one important dimension which this analysis of share price growth leaves out and that is dividend income – the cash which the shareholder receives between buying and selling the shares. This is clearly part of the value which the shareholder is receiving but will not be taken into account by a straight buying and selling comparison. Thus there has to be some way of adding in this element before a complete shareholder value calculation can be made.

Therefore the full shareholder value calculation for an individual buying and selling shares can be expressed as an equation which effectively represents the *cash flow* of the transaction:

> Price of shares when sold − Price of shares when bought + Dividends received = Shareholder value

This equation of shareholder value can clearly be applied to an individual buying and selling a particular share but it raises a number of problems if it becomes the basis for measurement of shareholder value for a total business. There are even more problems if it is then used to cascade down to individual units within that business. Nevertheless these problems should not obscure the fact that the above equation is the basis of assessment of company performance by shareholders and the increasingly sophisticated analysts who advise them. Cash is what they take into account because, in the stock markets, cash is king.

This is the reason why organisations like The Boots Company, which was one of the first to apply shareholder value principles throughout its businesses, use this definition of value creation for both external communication to the financial community and internal communication to its employees. It is why Unilever has used this definition as the foundation for recent fundamental changes in its approach to corporate performance measurement, again both externally and internally. This equation is the true measure of value.

THE PROBLEMS OF APPLYING THE SHAREHOLDER VALUE EQUATION TO MEASURE PERFORMANCE

The problems of applying this equation can be divided into those which exist at total corporate level and those which only become a problem when used internally to measure business unit or divisional performance.

The fundamental problems at corporate level are:

- How is the result of this equation expressed, as a percentage, as a money figure, as an index compared to others?

- How do we fix a timescale for opening and closing market values, particularly when many shares will have been bought some time ago and may be held almost indefinitely by some shareholders?

- How do we take into account the impact of the time value of money between buying and selling?

- How do we link this measure to conventional profit indicators like operating profit and earnings per share which are now part of most companies' existing performance measurement language and behaviour?

- How does this concept of shareholder value relate to the accounting concept of shareholders' funds, defined as share capital plus retained profits?

- How can this approach be applied to a business which is not publicly quoted, such as a private company or government-owned organisation?

These are key issues which are at the heart of this topic and will therefore be the subject of later chapters of the book. When trying to cascade down from total company measures to business unit performance, there are further additions to the list of problems which are even more difficult to resolve. For example:

- How can you simulate share price and dividend at the business unit level?

- How can this measure of shareholder value be converted into levers which operating managers can understand?

- How do we link the long-term strategic planning process to shareholder value?

- How do we monitor performance against short- and long-term plans?

These issues have to be resolved by the top management of every company which moves to shareholder value measures. They have to create a performance measurement system which is geared to shareholder value but is also well balanced, fully integrated and understood by all the key players in the business. We will now explore some of the areas of integration and balance which need to be achieved to gain the benefits which will come from successful implementation.

THE BENEFITS OF AN INTEGRATED AND BALANCED PERFORMANCE MEASUREMENT SYSTEM

If management develop a performance measurement system which is based on shareholder value and which has the right degree of integration and balance, the benefits will be felt throughout the organisation. They will lead to improved performance and higher motivation at all levels because everyone will have goals which are congruent with each other and are geared to the objectives which shareholders regard as important.

However, the achievement of the necessary integration and balance is a far more difficult process than the actual choice of shareholder value measures. Companies who use management consultants to advise them on the development of the 'perfect' performance measure should also insist that their responsibilities extend to these broader areas. This is often left to management to sort out and the consultants, in their desire to select a technically correct measure, may forget these other key issues of implementation.

So what are the areas of integration and balance which need to be achieved?

Integration of total company and business unit measures

Whatever measure is chosen for the company as a whole does not necessarily have to be used at business unit level in identical form; indeed this may be impractical and even undesirable. The key task is to create the right links between them so that, if all business unit targets are achieved, so will the total company performance target.

This is easy to say but much more difficult to achieve. If a company moves to a performance measure based on the definition of shareholder value described earlier, it is likely to have two key features: it will be geared to *future* rather than past performance and it will be closely related to *cash* generation. Yet the performance measures frequently used by organisations have precisely the opposite characteristics – they are geared to accounting concepts based on *historic* performance and are geared to *profit* rather than cash flow. Thus the implementation of shareholder value measures needs a complete rethink of how business unit performance is measured and how their managers are rewarded. If you believe in WYMIWYG it is no use expecting a new shareholder value measure to work unless it can be cascaded down via an integrated system which drives decisions at the operating level.

Balance between technical correctness and management understanding

It is not enough for this integration to be achieved in technical terms, it also needs to be understood and believed in by managers. This is the dimension which can often be overlooked by those who are more familiar with the language and the concepts. A good illustration of this danger is the following formula produced by a management consulting firm to arrive at business values:

$$= \ddot{\Sigma} \frac{EP}{(L + K_e)} + \ddot{\Sigma} \frac{B_{s-1} (L + K_e)}{(L + K_e)} + \ddot{\Sigma} \frac{B}{(L + K_e)}$$

There may be a place for such formulae in the detailed development of internal valuation models as will be described in Chapter 6. They are, however, likely to be counter-productive if used as part of the communication process to managers whose understanding and commitment is needed for successful implementation. There should therefore be a search for measures which are related to shareholder value but which also pass two other key tests: they are likely to be understood by managers and can be used by them for measurement and control purposes. This is why economic value added (or EVA) and similar measures have achieved such acceptance in recent years, not because they have a perfect link to shareholder value but because they have the closest links of all those measures which are relatively easily understood by managers and can be used to manage their business units. We will cover EVA in depth in Chapter 4.

This balance can also be influenced at the operational end by a carefully tailored programme of training for managers. Even when care is taken to simplify the chosen indicators as much as possible, there may still be difficult communication problems to overcome. For instance, the definition of shareholder value described earlier may seem relatively simple to communicate but the two underlying principles – the focus on future performance and the emphasis on cash – are totally opposite to the way in which managers are often conditioned to think. Thus the training objective has to be to change fundamentally all previously held assumptions.

Integration between long-term strategy and operational performance

This integration is a challenge for top management with any performance measurement system but it becomes even more vital when new measures related to shareholder value are introduced. And it is to a large extent an issue of communication. However brilliant the strategy and however closely it is linked to shareholder value, it will fail if the managers who deliver operational performance do not receive the proper communication. This communication must involve a conversion of strategic goals related to shareholder value into operational performance targets which can be closely monitored.

This issue is not just about overt communication to lower levels, it is also about consistent behaviour by top managers. It is not unusual for a top manager to attend a strategy meeting and agree new shareholder value measures but to continue to measure by the old familiar levers at the operational level. As the financial director of one of our clients, a large chemical company, said: 'EVA will only work when the CEO refers to that number rather than operating profit when he visits the divisions.'

Another big company, a well known major retailer, has an EVA figure in its reporting pack which nobody ever discusses because top management do not seem to understand how it is arrived at. Unless these kind of problems can be solved, even the most technically perfect system will founder.

Balance between challenging goals, realistic targets and required shareholder returns

Financial performance will not achieve required levels just because the best measures have been introduced. It will also not happen just because top management set challenging goals and put pressure on them to be achieved. Performance as measured by any indicator will only be achieved if the target is realistic in the first place and if there is a climate which is motivating to the managers who have to deliver.

Therefore it is not helpful for top management to set goals according to measures of shareholder value and then autocratically cascade down imposed targets based on what is necessary to achieve them. There has to be a careful assessment of the marketplace, the existing competitive position and the gaps between current performance and the required levels of achievement. If the gaps are too great in the short term but are achievable over a period of years, there must be a phased long-term plan to change the levers necessary to create the required shareholder value.

There may be occasions where market conditions and competitive position are never likely to lead to performance which creates shareholder value. In this situation the options for top management are stark and have to be considered in shareholder value terms. Do we sell the business, do we close it down, are there alternative strategies, or do we just carry on destroying value? As we will see in later chapters, the concept of shareholder value can provide the framework for such strategic decisions by evaluating the comparative present values for each strategy.

Balancing financial and non-financial measures

This final balance is perhaps the most important and should be clear at the beginning of any book on financial performance measurement. Financial measures are important but they are, in the end, only the way in which the score is kept. Successful performance is the result of a whole series of actions taken by managers in running the business, having regular contact with customers, motivating employees and setting up a wide range of systems and processes. However good the financial measure and however good current performance may be, the potential for future shareholder value can be lost if the more intangible and non-financial aspects of the business are forgotten.

Thus recent thinking, led by Robert Kaplan of the Harvard Business School, has suggested that managers should balance their financial performance measures by the parallel monitoring of non-financial indicators across three other dimensions – *customers, employees and processes*. There are some variations around this theme – other versions emphasise learning and innovation rather than processes in general – but the message is the same: running a business involves more than monitoring financial indicators, and long-term shareholder value will only come from simultaneous attention to these 'softer' areas.

The framework of the balanced scorecard is shown in Figure 1.1. The relationship of the balanced scorecard to shareholder value measures can be seen at two levels. First, it is a reminder that there are other things apart from financial measures which top management must monitor to create the right balance. Second, it can be a mechanism by which the concept of shareholder value is cascaded down.

Figure 1.1
FRAMEWORK FOR THE BALANCED SCORECARD

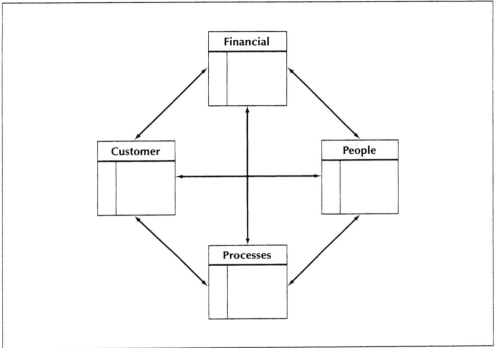

We have already stated that measures of shareholder value must be converted to drivers which operational managers can understand. As these are cascaded down, there will come a point where the measure does not necessarily have to be financial. The factory supervisor's contribution to shareholder value may be best measured by the yield percentage of materials in to materials out, the warehouse manager's contribution by days stock held, the sales person who does not control price or mix may be best measured by volume growth or market share.

We will return to the framework of the balanced business scorecard in the final chapter when we look at implementation in more depth. At the same time we will look at these issues of balance and integration again because they are at the heart of successful implementation of any system of shareholder value measurement.

In the meantime we need a full understanding of conventional financial performance measures. We need this for two reasons: first, to understand in more detail why they do not have a direct relationship to shareholder value; second, because they are the cornerstone of existing performance measurement systems for both internal and external reporting and must be the starting point for change. They are therefore the subject of the next two chapters.

2

Operational measures of business performance

> 'What gets measured gets managed.'
>
> G. Bennett Stewart III, Stern Stewart

Conventional accounting measures have recently been under attack from a number of directions and not only from those who advocate the principles of shareholder value. In a survey conducted by the *CFO* magazine (Birchard, 1995), 80 per cent of American companies acknowledged the need to improve their financial performance measurement systems. The article went on to say, 'Yesterday's accounting results say nothing about the factors that help grow market share and profits. Nor do traditional measurement systems help to assure senior management that workers in the field are actually carrying out corporate strategy.'

In spite of these criticisms and the desire for change, traditional financial performance measures still play a central role in corporate life. Even if companies are beginning to move towards new measures linked more directly to shareholder value, conventional accounting still has a major part to play in monitoring performance. Whatever its limitations, it is far too deeply linked to the legal and regulatory side of business for it to be completely replaced by new approaches.

Traditional accounting also provides the starting point for some of the measures of shareholder value which we will be covering later. The next two chapters will therefore review the key financial indicators which are derived from accounting principles and which are currently used by analysts inside and outside companies. We will also examine their strengths and weaknesses.

THE OBJECTIVES OF FINANCIAL ANALYSIS

Financial performance measures can be classified into two main areas which represent fundamentally different approaches to analysis:

- measures of performance which show how well a business is being run at the *operating* level, by analysis of both profitability and cash flow;

- measures of performance as seen from the *shareholder* point of view, again from both profitability and cash flow perspectives.

These two approaches are clearly linked but they have a fundamentally different focus. For instance, the operating approach would start with operating profit before interest and tax, whereas the shareholder approach would start with earnings after all such charges have been covered. Neither approach is right or wrong. It is just that the analysis process has a different focus and is asking different questions.

It is important to understand that the profitability ratios discussed in this chapter are all derived from figures which are based on accounting principles. They are not therefore linked to cash generation and this is one of the main reasons why there is not a direct relationship to the definition of shareholder value as described in Chapter 1. It also means that the ratios are only as good as the accounting principles used and there may be major problems of interpretation and comparison because of different accounting standards by country and by company. This is one reason why we try to complete the picture by covering cash flow measures at the end of each of the next two chapters.

The experienced analyst is therefore likely to use ratios carefully and sceptically, asking questions rather than hoping to obtain definite answers. This may indeed be one reason why there is a not a close correlation between accounting measures and shareholder value – the experienced analyst is too sophisticated to believe that increased profit should always justify a recommendation to buy a share. He or she will want to examine the accounting and the business issues before taking a view.

KEY OPERATIONAL MEASURES

Return on sales

The simplest and perhaps most widely used measure of operational performance, both inside and outside companies, is return on sales (ROS), also called profit margin. It is popular, perhaps too popular, because it is easy to calculate and the numbers all come from one document, the profit and loss account/income statement.

Using the most common terminology, the ROS equation looks like this:

$$\frac{\text{Operating profit}}{\text{Sales}} \times 100$$

It is expressed as a percentage and a 10 per cent ROS means that there is 10p profit for every pound of sales.

By operating profit we mean the profit after deducting all costs of operations, but before interest, tax or dividend. Other frequently used terms for the same level of profit are operating income and trading profit. This ratio is commonly monitored by managers as a key performance indicator and they will normally look for a high level and one which is improving. ROS effectively measures the added value which is being created by selling products for more than it costs to run the business. It can therefore be a powerful ratio for comparing progress and competitive position.

As an indicator for management it has an important place but, for the shareholder, it has a number of weaknesses. For instance:

- It takes no account of the investment required to generate the sales, either from shareholders or from borrowing.

- It may be invalid to compare ROS margins between different businesses, even within the same sector. A typical margin for a supermarket would be 5 per cent, yet for a department store over 10 per cent. Comparing a supermarket with a pharmaceuticals company, where margins are often over 20 per cent, would be even less valid.

- It does not provide a complete view of management performance. It is only part of the picture because it looks solely at the profit and loss account, ignoring both balance sheet and cash flow. Managers can allow stocks or debtors to be high and capital investment to be uncontrolled, yet their margin could still look good.

- As an operating measure it ignores all the areas of management below the operating level, particularly interest and tax.

- An increase in ROS does not necessarily correlate to the creation of shareholder value.

Return on capital employed

Return on capital employed (ROCE) is a more valid and complete measure of operational performance. Its greater validity arises from the fact that, unlike ROS, it relates the profit generated by the business to the resources invested. It therefore has a much closer relationship to shareholder value though, as it too is an operating rather than a shareholder measure, the correlation can never be perfect.

This measure has many variations and many labels, the most common being return on capital (ROC), return on net assets (RONA) and return on investment (ROI). Different companies and analysts tend to tailor the definition to meet their specific needs and it would be impossible to go into all the variations.

The basic ROCE equation looks like this:

$$\frac{\text{Operating profit}}{\text{Capital employed}} \times 100$$

The result is expressed as a percentage and generally speaking, the higher it is, the more effectively managers have been using the assets which have been invested in their business.

We have already covered the definition of operating profit and it should be noted that this is the same level of profit as used for the calculation of return on sales. The link provided by this common factor will be developed later.

It is in the definition of capital employed that there is most variation and potential for confusion. It is possible to arrive at a capital employed figure from either side of the balance sheet but it is easier for managers to understand and apply if it is taken from an asset base.

Capital employed is therefore best extracted from the assets side of the balance sheet and can be most simply defined as:

> Capital employed equals Fixed assets plus Stock plus Debtors less Creditors

The critical factor with any ratio definition is that the component parts are logical and consistent with each other, bearing in mind the question which that ratio is asking. The ROCE ratio is asking the question, 'What return is this company making on its operations in relation to the assets which management are using to run the business?' If we are taking operating profit as one part of this ratio, we therefore need to take the assets *which are being used in operations* for the other part.

Thus assets like cash and investments in shares would not be included in capital employed, first because they are not usually managed directly by those involved in operations, and second – the most crucial point – the income from these assets would not be included in a normal definition of operating profit.

We deduct creditors from capital employed because that is interest-free credit which management are using to reduce the investment required from external sources. Thus the use of creditor finance can be an important means of influencing the ROCE.

We have used the general terms debtors and creditors to make the definition short and simple. To be complete and consistent these headings should be extended to include any current asset or current liability relating to operations; for example debtors should include prepayments and creditors should include provisions and accruals. In fact the definition could be broadened to replace debtors and creditors with 'current assets and current liabilities relating to operations'.

Managers who are targeted on ROCE are encouraged to see life in simple terms. Success is about making as much profit as possible – nothing new here – but also about minimising the investment in assets. This means reducing capital expenditure and/or selling off fixed assets which are surplus to requirements. However, as these are decisions which are often difficult to take in the short term, the pressure to improve ROCE often focuses attention on the more controllable areas of stock, debtors and creditors, commonly referred to collectively as working capital. Reducing stock, collecting cash more quickly and taking more credit from suppliers are frequently the actions of managers who are measured by ROCE, particularly at the end of the accounting period!

As there are strong links between ROCE and EVA which is to be covered in Chapter 4, we need to understand both the strengths and the weaknesses of ROCE – the strengths which made it the most effective measure used by many top companies in the 1970s and 1980s; the weaknesses which have caused many companies more recently to reject it in favour of EVA.

Strengths

- ROCE combines variables from both the balance sheet and profit and loss account, thus giving it a significant advantage over ROS and other ratios to sales.

- There should be some relationship between improving ROCE and cash generation. The actions required to improve ROCE – increase profit and reduce assets – are both likely to produce positive cash flow, and, as we saw in Chapter 1, cash flow is what delivers shareholder value.

- Once they understand the concept, it is relatively easy for managers to see the need for this ratio to be high. They can relate it to the normal rules of investment: 'People have invested money to buy assets for us, we need to deliver a return which covers the cost of money and the risk involved.' They can understand why a return below (say) 10 per cent is unlikely to be enough to cover interest, tax and required shareholder return.

- ROCE can be cascaded down to incorporate return on sales and a range of other operational ratios, using a powerful hierarchy which we will explore later.

Weaknesses

The weaknesses to some extent depend on the purpose for which the ratio is being used. If the ROCE ratio were to be used to compare companies in different sectors with different accounting standards, this list of weaknesses would be far longer. But that would be a naive and inappropriate use of ROCE. Even assuming that the ratio is being used appropriately, there are still a number of key weaknesses:

- The problems of asset valuation can make the results misleading. The accounting standards in most countries encourage the use of the principle of historical cost to value assets. In times of inflation this can cause businesses which purchased fixed assets many years ago to appear artificially profitable. Many companies try to resolve this issue by revaluation to market or replacement cost but this increases the areas of judgement and complexity. It also requires regular and costly updating to be useful.

- An additional and highly controversial accounting issue which affects the validity of many ROCE comparisons is the treatment of acquired goodwill – whether or not this item should be considered as part of the asset base. The accounting standards vary in different countries and in different companies. Some companies may exclude it from their published accounts to harmonise with country accounting standards but still bring it into the calculation for internal control purposes. This point makes it clear that the definition of ratios is much more than an accounting matter, there are behavioural implications too. The question which should be asked here is: 'Do we want our managers to be accountable for money spent on acquisitions in past years, or do we focus on what they can control today?' The answer will be a management rather than accounting judgement but it will also have an impact on the assessment of the percentage ROCE achieved, in both absolute and comparative terms.

- A major criticism of ROCE, and the one which is felt to be the biggest concern in relation to shareholder value, is that it does not encourage managers to grow a business; in fact it can do exactly the opposite. If the company regards the most successful division as the one which produces the highest percentage ROCE, the WYMIWYG principle will ensure that this is what their managers will deliver. Yet this may not be in the interests of the business and in line with shareholder value generation. The ROCE could be increased in percentage terms by a strategy which reduces investment and destroys the future of the business. Or good value-creation opportunities could be rejected on the grounds that the percentage will be reduced. This is one of the strongest arguments in favour of replacing ROCE by EVA and will be developed further in Chapter 4.

- Though ROCE has many strengths, it is just not appropriate for certain types of business. The emphasis on tangible assets as a key area of management control is simply not helpful to the manager of an advertising agency or consultancy firm. The key assets of these businesses are likely to be their people and conventional accounting does not reflect these in the asset base. Therefore operating profit in money terms is likely to be as effective (or ineffective) a measure as ROCE and alternatives like profit per employee or even return on sales may be more relevant and more motivating.

- Finally, and this is the key issue, there is no strong correlation between ROCE and shareholder value. This is not surprising when we think of the context and purpose of ROCE – as an operating measure. It was never intended for shareholder value measurement and the very fact that it starts with pre-tax, pre-interest profits makes such a correlation unlikely. For instance, the low performing company at the operating level could still produce good returns to shareholders by effective tax management.

The cascading power of ROS and ROCE – asset turnover

Despite their weaknesses, return on sales and return on capital employed have some good things going for them, particularly when they are linked together. They are bound to be linked because they both use operating profit as their driver. Together they can provide a cascading framework which helps managers to control the business, and this comes from a third ratio which provides that powerful linkage – the asset turnover.

Asset turnover is a multiple of sales to capital employed. It tells management how effectively they are using their assets. A business which has a high asset turnover – for example, one which has sales of 10 to capital employed of 1, a multiple of 10 – would be using its assets well, turning them over effectively. Another way of thinking about this is that the business requires a small amount of assets for every pound of sales and some analysts express the ratio that way round, as 10 per cent capital employed to sales.

As with return on sales, the level of asset turnover depends very much on the type of business and cannot be looked at in isolation. It is the interaction with ROS to produce the ROCE number which should be the subject of analysis and this will be entirely dependent on sector and strategy.

This interaction can be shown by these three linking equations:

$$\frac{\text{Operating profit}}{\text{Sales}} \times \frac{\text{Sales}}{\text{Capital employed}} = \frac{\text{Operating profit}}{\text{Capital employed}}$$

OR

Return on sales $\times$ Asset turnover $=$ Return on capital employed

From a management point of view, these linking equations make it clear that it is not enough to make a high return on sales or to make a high asset turnover. The important thing is that the two together interact to produce an effective return on capital employed. For instance, a discount supermarket might make a return on sales of only 2 per cent, yet by keeping assets to a minimum (maybe by leasing all its properties and driving stocks down) it could produce an asset turnover of 10 times, thus delivering 20 per cent ROCE. Another company in a capital-intensive business like telecommunications might make the same ROCE of 20 per cent, yet would achieve this by a 20 per cent ROS and an asset turnover of only 1.

These three ratios form the basis for the powerful framework of the hierarchy of ratios, originally accredited to Dupont and later used by a number of major companies, notably GEC. Its power is in its ability to start from ROCE, cascade down to ROS and asset turnover and then go even further down to the operating measures which individual managers can control. A generic version of the hierarchy is shown in Figure 2.1.

This framework is powerful at a number of levels. First, it is as a way of showing managers how their decisions feed in to ROCE, how their operational actions regarding stock or gross margin have an impact on overall company performance. This thinking can be helpful even for companies which have rejected ROCE for other measures like EVA because the hierarchy still contains many of the decision areas which drive shareholder value. A measure does not have to be technically perfect to be useful for management; a key benefit of the hierarchy is that it provokes a positive response from the vast majority of managers who see it. A number of ratios which had previously seemed unconnected now come together.

Figure 2.1
HIERARCHY OF RATIOS

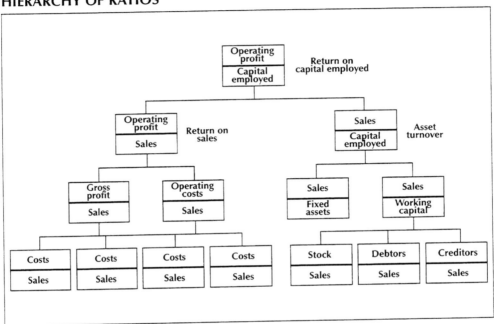

The hierarchy is also a valuable framework for an integrated approach to analysis and then to action. Top management can start by asking why ROCE has increased or declined, then cascade down to split that change between ROS and asset turnover. Changes at that level can then be further explored via profit and loss analysis on the left and balance sheet analysis on the right.

This enables trade-offs between decision-making variables to be seen clearly – for example, a discount to customers which reduces margin on the left but improves debtors on the right, or an investment in capital which makes asset turnover worse but reduces the cost base. This is the answer to those who are concerned about profit and loss myopia – the impact on the drivers of value which are in the balance sheet can be seen in an integrated way.

One final benefit of the hierarchy is its strong link to cash flow generation. If all the ratios in the hierarchy move the right way, cash is likely to be generated. On the right-hand side, improvement may come from asset reduction, in which case the impact on cash will be positive. On the left an improvement in margins will also generate cash, all things being equal. The key weaknesses in terms of correlation to cash and shareholder value are the potential discouragement to growth which was discussed earlier and the lack of focus on tax. It could therefore be argued that ROCE has a lot going for it and is perhaps unfairly derided. If combined with tax and growth objectives, it is a powerful management tool.

CASH FLOW ANALYSIS – THE OPERATIONAL PERSPECTIVE

One question which the reader may understandably ask is this. If, as we said in the first chapter, cash is king, why don't we just take cash flow measures? Why bother with these imperfect ratios of profitability? Why not go direct to the only measure which shareholders care about?

To answer this question we need to go back to the basic reasons why accounting, despite all its imperfections, is necessary to manage any business. It is true that cash is the only real measure but that applies in the very long term. In the short term, a week, a month, a year, cash is a poor measure of how well a business is performing. A negative cash flow can occur during a very successful year if there has been a large investment in capital expenditure. There can be a positive cash flow for a period if stocks have been run down, followed by a negative cash flow in the next period when they are replaced. Profit measurement equalises the impact of these factors by matching the sales of a period with the costs of running the business for that same period, thus providing management and shareholders with a better measure of short-term performance.

Despite the weaknesses of cash flow as a short-term measure of performance, a report on cash movements has become a familiar part of most reporting systems. At the simplest level, cash flow statements are merely recordings of cash in and cash out, the movements in the bank account. However, a more complex but, once understood, more valuable approach is to use a format which works back from profit to arrive at cash flow.

At the operating level the structure of such a cash flow statement would appear as in Figure 2.2, in which a few simple numbers illustrate the relationships.

Figure 2.2
CASH FLOW STATEMENT – OPERATING LEVEL

Operating profit		100
Add back Depreciation		10
		110
Increase in working capital:		
Increased stock	(12)	
Increased debtors	(15)	
Increased creditors	8	
		(19)
Cash flow before capital expenditure		91
Capital expenditure		(52)
Net cash flow from operations		39

This style of statement arrives at real cash flow but via the back-door route. It starts with profit and then shows all the differences between profit and cash which bring the final answer back to cash flow. Depreciation is added back because it is not a cash flow and the answer (110 above) is effectively the profit as if no depreciation had been charged. This level is often loosely called cash flow in some circles but there are other adjustments needed to arrive at the real cash number.

The working capital adjustment is required because the profit and loss account does not take such movements into account. The level of cash flow after working capital changes (91 above) is an important one for management to monitor. If there is a negative number at that stage, it means that the business is not generating enough profit from its operations even to cover working capital growth. This level can be called OCF or operating cash flow though that term is also used by some companies to describe the final bottom line.

This final cash flow number (39 above) represents the movement in the bank account caused by operations and, in principle, should link to the opening and closing bank balances. However, in practice, there will be other non-operational items which also affect cash (for example, tax and dividend) and which need to be adjusted for a final reconciliation.

This cash flow reporting structure shows clearly the link between profit and cash flow which is vital to the understanding of shareholder value measurement. It shows that there are relatively few levers which need to be controlled if profit is to be converted into cash flow. If we net depreciation off against capital expenditure to arrive at a net fixed asset investment figure (42 above), the relationship can be further simplified in the form of this equation:

> Profit (100) plus or minus Working capital change (19), plus or minus
> Fixed asset change (42) equals Net cash flow from operations (39)

This equation leaves out a number of other possible factors (like asset disposal, acquisitions, other current asset and liability changes) and the inclusion of these variables often blinds management to the simplicity of the linkage.

Though cash flow is usually expressed and discussed in money terms, there are certain ratios based on cash flow which are used within some companies. Net cash flow as a percentage of operating profit is quite popular, effectively saying, 'how much of that profit is being generated in cash terms?' Net cash flow as a percentage of capital employed is also used by some – 'what return are we getting in *cash* on what we've invested?'

All these measures will be of interest to shareholders but it will be interest only. These ratios are measuring operating performance and are therefore primarily for management control, for comparisons with competitors, for analysis of trends of cost and asset efficiency. The next chapter has a significantly different focus: the ratios which have evolved to become the traditional indicators of performance for shareholders. Their interest has been at the bottom line.

3

Shareholder ratios

'For the last fifty years ... the financial community has been obsessed with the income statement and its all-important bottom-line figures, net income and earnings per share.'

Barbara S. Thomas, Commissioner SEC

A number of the measures in this chapter have been attacked in recent times as being imperfect or even misleading, yet still they form the basis of much analysis by shareholders and those who advise them. Old habits die hard and, though there is general acceptance that few of these measures correlate well to the definition of shareholder value shown in Chapter 1, they are still in general use. It should also be stressed that a measure does not have to be perfect to be useful, as long as the limitations are well understood.

Shareholder ratios can be divided into two types: those which are extracted purely from published accounts and those which show relationships between accounting numbers and stock market values. This first category has three main ratios, all of which are important.

RETURN ON EQUITY

Return on equity (ROE) is the equivalent of return on capital employed but from a shareholder point of view. Its calculation is as follows:

$$\frac{\text{Earnings}}{\text{Shareholders' equity}} \times 100$$

This ratio starts with the annual earnings, the profit after interest, tax and all appropriations other than ordinary dividends – what is left for the shareholders. It then relates this bottom-line profit to the equity, the amount of cumulative share capital and retained profits which have been invested ever since the company was formed.

This latter number clearly has little relevance to a shareholder who has bought shares in today's stock market because the market value is likely to be very different from equity in the balance sheet, a point we will develop later. Perhaps it is better to see return on equity as the measure for shareholders who have been with the company right from the start. They have invested share capital and have also allowed the directors to retain profit in the business rather than paying dividends.

For those companies which are not quoted on the Stock Exchange, there is a stronger argument for using ROE as a key measure of main board performance and many do. The equity represents the total amount which the directors have been given by shareholders to use in the business and the earnings number shows what they are delivering at the bottom line.

ROE has, however, become devalued in recent times for three reasons. First, the same accounting problems as bedevil the ROCE measure also have an adverse impact on the usefulness of ROE, particularly the under-valuation of fixed assets and the differing treatments of goodwill. Second, in public companies the emphasis is much more on share value in the stock market and ROE does not take account of this, as indeed it was never intended to do. Third, the evidence of recent research is that, contrary to earlier beliefs, the correlation between ROE and shareholder value as described in Chapter 1 is low compared to other measures.

EARNINGS PER SHARE

Earnings per share (EPS) is still the most quoted and widely used measure, even though it cannot be compared across companies except in terms of relative growth. Its calculation is simple, and the formula is:

$$\frac{\text{Earnings}}{\text{Average shares in issue during the year}}$$

This ratio is showing the amount of bottom-line profit being delivered to a shareholder with one share, either in dividend or as retained profits. It means nothing in comparison to other companies because the number of shares is a unique characteristic of each company, based on its history and its capital structure.

The pressure from the stock market is to grow the EPS number year on year in relation to growth achieved in the past and by other companies. The fact that analysts focus on EPS rather than looking at earnings in money terms puts pressure on management to think carefully about the issue of new shares lest the EPS should be diluted. It also means that options to increase EPS by reducing the number of shares (for example, by share buyback) should be considered by any management which wishes to please its shareholders.

There is no doubt that EPS has been a key factor in driving share prices in the past and was, until this decade, seen as the measure which stock market analysts looked at before all others. It was also number one on the list of measures which main boards of public companies used to judge success. It is only in recent times that research has questioned the correlation to shareholder value and other measures have been found to relate more closely to it.

One other benefit of EPS is that, when related to share price, it gives valuable comparative information about the market's view of the company, as we shall see later in this chapter.

DIVIDEND COVER

This is the third and final measure to be derived purely from company results. It is an important one for those shareholders who look for dividend. The dividend cover measures the proportion of earnings which is paid out in dividend and therefore also shows, by implication, the amount retained.

The formula is as follows:

$$\frac{\text{Earnings}}{\text{Dividend}}$$

It is usually expressed as a multiple though it is reversed, converted to a percentage and called the payout ratio in some circles, particularly in the USA. A dividend cover of 2 means that half the profit has been paid in cash to shareholders and therefore the other half retained. Alternatively the payout ratio is 50 per cent.

This measure is of vital interest to shareholders, particularly for year-on-year comparisons. They are able to see whether they are getting the same proportion of earnings in cash. For some shareholders a high cover/low payout may be acceptable and even desirable, depending on their tax position and their need for short-term cash. Whatever their preference, the dividend cover ratio helps them to monitor the trend.

Acceptable or normal levels depend entirely on the industrial sector – the more the need for growth and future investment, the higher the cover (and the lower the payout) is likely to be.

RATIOS FROM STOCK MARKET INFORMATION – MARKET CAPITALISATION

Ratios derived from stock market information are completely different to those from published financial information. They change every day as market prices change and they measure external factors as well as accounting numbers. They are therefore much less easy to manipulate as it is the market which determines one of the variables.

Before we examine these measures we need to define an important concept for shareholder value analysis – *market capitalisation.*

Market capitalisation is the total value of all shares in the stock market and is calculated as follows:

Total shares issued × Current share price

This is a critical number for the assessment of shareholder value because it is as close as you will get to the total market value of a company at any one time. It becomes the starting point for takeover negotiations concerning public companies because it represents the value of what the shareholders have already.

It is also useful to relate this number to the shareholders' equity as defined earlier. Equity is made up of share capital plus retained profits – the amount put in by the shareholders. The amount by which the market capitalisation exceeds the equity can be seen as *the value which the management of the company has added*. It also represents the goodwill a buyer would have to pay if an acquisition took place at the current share price. We will see in Chapter 5 that this excess is similar in principle to what is often referred to as MVA or market value added, now regarded by many as a key measure of shareholder value. Figure 3.1 shows this relationship of equity to market capitalisation.

Figure 3.1
RELATIONSHIP BETWEEN EQUITY AND MARKET CAPITALISATION

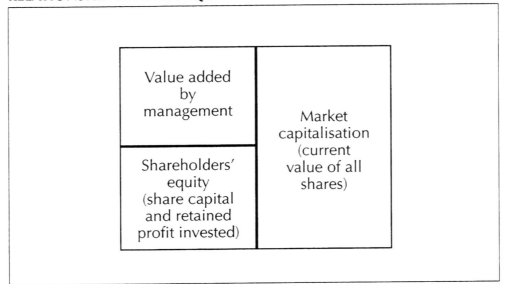

It should be emphasised that the extent to which this gap represents real value added depends on the accounting conventions used to arrive at equity. All the reservations which we applied earlier to ROCE and ROE are also likely to distort this gap. Apparent value added could be no more than undervalued fixed assets. Thus a true definition of 'market value added' needs to adjust for these factors and this issue will also be explored in Chapter 5.

PRICE TO BOOK RATIO

The extent to which the market capitalisation exceeds shareholders' equity can also be expressed as a ratio. The price to book (also known as market to book) ratio is calculated as follows:

$$\frac{\text{Market capitalisation}}{\text{Shareholders' equity}}$$

It is usually expressed as a multiple rather than a percentage and the higher it is the better from a shareholder value point of view. Like many ratios, however, it is impossible to draw definite conclusions without relating to the sector norm. For instance, a successful advertising agency would have a high multiple because of its low need for tangible asset investment. What can be stated with confidence is that a number close to 1.0 is a sign that a company has not performed well for its shareholders. Little value has been added. This ratio is more popular in the USA than Europe where it is sometimes reversed to become a percentage of equity to market capitalisation.

PRICE EARNINGS RATIO

The price earnings ratio (or P/E multiple) is perhaps the most widely quoted comparative measure on the Stock Exchange. It is calculated like this:

$$\frac{\text{Current share price}}{\text{Earnings per share}}$$

The P/E multiple provides a measure of the extent to which today's share price – which reflects all available information and future expectations – exceeds the most recent year's earnings. It relates future to past and is therefore a measure of the strength of the forces – apart from EPS itself – which drive share values. The higher the P/E, the stronger are the future expectations; these will be a combination of general economic conditions, factors in the industrial sector and special features of the company itself. The higher the P/E the more the market expects a company to get better in relation to its current EPS performance – this may show confidence in the quality of management, but on the other hand it may merely reflect the poor quality of present performance.

Like most ratios P/Es are best expressed in relative terms, in relation to the sector average and to the market as a whole. A high P/E ratio tends to be good for existing shareholders who have already shared in the capital growth which has caused it, but not so good for shareholders who wish to buy today. For them the P/E is merely confirming that you pay a high price for something which is expected to do well. If an investor buys and retains a share with a P/E of 50 – a sign of a company with great expectations – it also means that if profits do not improve, there will only be a 2 per cent return, even if all profits are paid as dividend.

DIVIDEND YIELD

The final shareholder ratio in our coverage is the dividend yield. This is calculated as follows:

$$\frac{\text{Dividend per share}}{\text{Current share price}} \times 100$$

The dividend yield is expressed as a percentage and is of particular interest to the shareholder who is looking for a cash return. As was shown above, however, the better the reputation of the share, the lower that yield will be. The other factor which drives dividend yield is the proportion of payout as measured by the dividend cover.

It is not unusual for a share with the combined characteristics of a high P/E and low payout to have a return below 2 per cent. Conversely a high yield often indicates a business which is paying out cash now due to the limited future growth prospects and lack of opportunities to invest in projects that earn above the cost of capital.

It would be wrong to discount the importance of dividend yield on the assumption that investors are only in the stock market to achieve capital gain. There are shareholders who are more interested in immediate income than capital growth and, for them, the dividend yield is of major importance. For all shareholders it is part of their overall assessment of the value of holding that share.

CASH FLOW

Before we leave shareholder measures, we must mention cash flow as seen from the shareholder perspective. In the previous chapter we looked at the calculation of operational cash flow from a starting point of operating profit, working back to cash by adjustment for asset movements. Stock market analysts adopt a similar approach but their perspective causes them to examine the company's full cash flow generation rather than purely operating items. Such analysis is increasingly being carried out by the more sophisticated analysts and their goal is to arrive at what they call *free cash flow*.

The detailed methods of getting there will differ but the objective is the same: to find out how much cash is being generated before those distributions of profit which are discretionary – in other words, to see what is potentially available for shareholders. This is similar in principle to the cash flow calculation at the operating level in Chapter 2, but here the starting point is the shareholders' bottom line.

A typical route to free cash flow, widely adopted by US analysts, is shown in Figure 3.2, with some simple numbers to show the relationships.

Figure 3.2
TYPICAL ROUTE TO FREE CASH FLOW

Earnings (after interest, tax and all appropriations)	100
Add back Depreciation and other non-cash items	25
	125
Increase in working capital (stock, debtors, creditors)	(50)
	75
Capital expenditure	(60)
Free cash flow	15

The intelligent analyst would not draw too many conclusions from one year because capital expenditure needs are likely to be volatile from year to year in many cases. Some take a 'normalised' figure for capital, trying to arrive at a typical annual spend over the long term. One grey area is whether acquisitions should be deducted, as their impact is effectively the same as capital expenditure. The answer will depend on whether acquisitions are likely to be a regular part of the long-term strategy.

The objective of this type of analysis is to find out whether the business is generating enough cash to provide future value for its shareholders. A low or negative projection for the future is a danger signal which would cause concern about future dividend and growth, thus adversely affecting the share price.

This emphasis on cash rather than profit is all part of the tendency of the more sophisticated stock market analysts to have reservations about the usefulness of conventional accounting measures. During the late 1980s and early 1990s these opinion formers became increasingly concerned that the management of many companies did not have the same view. Despite general statements of the need to generate cash and create shareholder value, earnings per share and return on capital employed continued to be regarded as the key measures by many management teams. Cash and the return they were providing to shareholders still seemed to take second place.

What was needed was a measure that could be easily related to the familiar profit-based indicators, yet still had a close link to cash generation and shareholder value. Economic value added or EVA came along at the right time to answer this call and became so popular among analysts that the mere announcement of its introduction could cause a share price to rise.

In the next chapter we will examine its nature, its benefits and how far it meets the need to correlate with real shareholder value.

4

Economic value added

'The only question to ask managers is, are we adding EVA? All other measures are like layers of paint on the *Queen Mary* – we are having to scrape them off to save the ship from sinking.'

G. Bennett Stewart III, Stern Stewart

In Chapters 2 and 3 we looked at some of the traditional financial measures used to assess business performance. The limitation of most of these measures is that they are derived from accounting figures and are therefore only as good as the accounting principles used. And as accounting principles do not necessarily reflect shareholder value, there is frequently little correlation to share price, the key driver of shareholder return.

A further serious weakness is the fact that many measures do not reflect the complete set of variables which drive *long-term* value creation. For example, ROCE has long been viewed as one of the more effective measures used by top companies yet its use can encourage managers to adopt strategies which are detrimental to the business over the long term. For example, a reduction in capital expenditure will invariably improve short-term ROCE but could adversely affect long-term growth prospects.

It is as a result of these limitations that managers, consultants and analysts have been searching for a new type of performance measure that will be more closely aligned to corporate strategies and long-term value creation. As the CFO of Monsanto recently stated: 'We needed to find a financial metric that would create new levels of share owner value by being more directly correlated with stock price. It had to be a measure that's economically based and tied to cash flows, rather than accountancy based.'

In order to meet their number one priority of maximising shareholder value, companies like Coca-Cola, Microsoft and Unilever are leading their businesses away from conventional indicators like ROS, ROCE and ROE towards more value-based measures. New measures and acronyms are being heard in the offices of financial directors and City analysts. To be credible managers now need to understand, among others, total shareholder return (TSR), cash flow return on investment (CFROI), market value added (MVA) and economic value added (EVA). The objective of the next three chapters is to review these new metrics and assess their strengths and weaknesses. Our starting point is EVA – a measure of profit which is becoming generally accepted as a short-term performance indicator which has a strong correlation to long-term shareholder value.

WHAT IS EVA?

The basic idea of economic value added (EVA) is not new. Despite all the recent attention, it is, at a fundamental level, the same concept as residual income which was first used earlier this century by General Motors. The acronym EVA was developed in the 1980s and later trademarked by Stern Stewart, a New York firm of management consultants. Since this time several other companies and consultants have adopted the same type of measure but have given it their own name. One hears mention, for instance, of economic profit, shareholder value added, economic earnings and trading contribution. One company – Pentland – has found an ingenious way of overcoming the terminology problem by inventing 'VAP' – value added to Pentland – as their internal indicator. All of these measures are fundamentally the same, though with important differences in the detailed calculations. To avoid confusion we will adopt the term EVA for the remainder of this chapter.

HOW TO DERIVE EVA

EVA overcomes some of the weaknesses of conventional accounting by creating a new concept of economic profit. As mentioned above, some companies actually use this term 'economic profit' to describe their own version of EVA. By economic profit we mean the difference between the sales made in a period and the real up-to-date cost of all resources consumed in that same period. A perfect calculation of economic profit would ensure that these resources are valued in true economic terms, reflecting current rather than historic costs. In practice some definitions of EVA do this more effectively than others.

It is, however, in its treatment of the economic cost of using assets within the business that EVA is significantly different from the measures described in the last two chapters. The key feature of EVA is that it brings balance sheet and therefore cash flow variables into the profit and loss account in a way which achieves the benefits of ROCE without some of the problems. It does this by charging the company's cost of capital as a percentage of assets employed in the business as a final entry before the bottom-line profit.

Another important feature of EVA is its emphasis on post-tax profit rather than profit at the operating level, encouraging managers to take a proactive approach to the management of this line of the profit and loss account. Not every company may wish to take this approach and we have seen companies adopt measures for their business units which are otherwise similar to EVA but at the pre-tax level. Their view is that it is better to encourage operating managers to leave tax issues to the specialists in the centre.

Therefore the basic definition of EVA is simple:

EVA = Post-tax profit less a charge on capital employed

The post-tax profit number is not as easy to extract as it may seem and this is one of the practical complexities of arriving at a true EVA number. The normal accounting definition of post tax profit – the earnings number in the profit and loss account – is after the deduction of interest costs. As the above charge on capital employed includes the cost of interest in the overall cost of capital calculation, an adjustment has to be made to avoid double counting. The actual interest cost is therefore added back and a new calculation of tax made on the adjusted profit. The resulting number is often called NOPAT – net operating profit after tax.

This adding back of interest may be an area of complexity but it illustrates a very important point. Interest on borrowing is not the only element of cost of capital which has to be charged to arrive at a true definition of economic profit. There is also the required return for shareholders and any inclusion of a charge for capital must reflect both elements. Thus interest is added back only to be included as part of the composite cost of capital figure.

The charge on capital employed is calculated as follows:

> Capital employed × Weighted average cost of capital

We stated in Chapter 2 that, when calculating ROCE, there are many variations of the definition of capital employed. We suggested that the simplest and most easily understood definition is *Fixed assets plus Stock plus Debtors less Creditors* and this applies equally to the calculation of EVA. The charge should reflect the cost of financing the net cost of those assets which have been used for business operations.

The weighted average cost of capital (WACC) is the average cost of debt and equity, weighted according to the proportions of the two types of finance. The precise calculation of WACC will be explored in more detail later in this chapter.

To demonstrate the concept of EVA Figure 4.1 provides a simple example.

Figure 4.1
SIMPLE CALCULATION OF EVA

Company A		
Capital employed		£100
Post-tax profit		£30
Weighted average cost of capital		10%
	£	
Post-tax profit	30	
Less Charge for capital employed		
(£100 × 10%)	(10)	
Economic value added (EVA)	£20	

The simplest way to see the bottom-line EVA number is that it represents what is left for shareholders after all costs have been covered, including the cost of borrowing and their own required return. A positive number means that value has been created; a negative number means that value has been destroyed. We will see later in this chapter and in Chapter 6 that it is not quite as simple as this but, at a fundamental level, this is how managers should be encouraged to think.

An alternative way of calculating EVA is to use what is known as the 'spread' method. This involves taking the excess of the ROCE over the cost of capital and applying it to the capital employed number. This has the advantage of relating EVA more closely to ROCE and also makes it clear that there is no real return until the cost of capital has been covered. Using this method the calculation of the same answer would be derived from the formula:

$$\text{EVA} = (\text{ROCE} - \text{Weighted average cost of capital}) \times \text{Capital employed}$$

Using the figures above, the ROCE is 30 per cent (£30 post-tax profit as a percentage of £100 capital employed) *less* 10 per cent WACC leaving a 20 per cent spread. When applied to the capital employed of £100, this gives an EVA of £20.

Another way of thinking about this 20 per cent spread is that it is the 'economic ROCE', the return being made in excess of the cost of capital. Some companies use it in this way and it can be a helpful indicator, though it still suffers from the same limitation as conventional ROCE – as a percentage measure it does not encourage maximisation of value in money terms.

OTHER ADJUSTMENTS TO ARRIVE AT ECONOMIC PROFIT

If EVA is to become a true measure of shareholder value, it has to do more than merely deduct a charge for cost of capital. Yet measures in many companies which are labelled EVA or economic profit do no more than make this one adjustment. Yet a fundamental problem remains – all the numbers above that line are still based on accounting concepts, many of which are contrary to our earlier definition of economic profit.

Stern Stewart has identified a possible 164 adjustments which can be applied to the profit or capital employed numbers before arriving at EVA. Some of these are described as behavioural, reflecting a desire to influence management actions in certain ways depending on strategic priorities. This confirms that the calculation of EVA is an inexact science and is, as we discussed in Chapter 1, an issue which goes beyond financial implications.

We will now focus on those adjustments which, while having behavioural implications, are primarily designed to align accounting profit more closely to economic reality. The more common adjustments to arrive at a truer definition of economic profit are as follows:

- **Capitalising research and development expenses and depreciating them over future periods.** The normal accounting convention is to treat such expenditure as an expense in the profit and loss account in the year it is incurred, a method which does not normally reflect economic reality. If a division/company has to absorb an unusual amount of R&D in one year this will reduce profits and hence EVA. By spreading the costs and matching them to future income, this adjustment creates a truer definition of profit and also encourages management to maintain investment in R&D. This adjustment is most necessary and effective when the pattern of spending on R&D is uneven.

- **Adding acquired goodwill into the capital employed number, where this practice is not followed in normal accounting policies.** The controversial issue of the accounting treatment of goodwill was addressed in Chapter 2 when we asked the question 'do we want our managers to be accountable for money spent on acquisitions in prior years?' If goodwill is included in the definition of capital employed, managers are made accountable for the cost of financing businesses that have been purchased in the past. It could be argued that, however demotivating, this is a reflection of economic reality and should be considered in any assessment of shareholder value.

- **Capitalising marketing costs in branded businesses and depreciating them over several years,** when the benefit of the investment is likely to be realised. The logic for this adjustment is similar to R&D and is also only justified where there are substantial non-recurring investments.

- **Changing the method of depreciation.** In their normal financial accounts the majority of companies use the straight line method based on historical cost, with no further charges once the asset has been fully written off. There are some companies – for instance,

Unilever and Philips – who use a different method of depreciation for internal management accounting to reflect the economic use of these assets. This involves indexing to current costs and making a notional charge for all assets in use at today's values. Where this kind of system is in use, the EVA number would obviously be based on the profit after these adjustments. If this kind of sophistication is not available, companies have to take a view on the best type of adjustment to make. Many choose not to bother because of the cost of obtaining accurate data on current costs and the complexity that is created. If so they are accepting that the profit and EVA numbers may be overstating true value creation.

- **Capitalising leases and treating them as if the assets had been purchased and the money borrowed.** Accounting principles already require this adjustment to be carried out for 'financial leases' – those which are in reality borrowing transactions by another name. This adjustment extends the principle to all leases, arguing that they are all ways of financing assets used in the business.

THE ISSUE OF UNDERSTANDABILITY AND CREDIBILITY

We stated in Chapter 1 that a good performance measure is one can that be easily understood by those managers striving to achieve it. A target that involves 164 adjustments will fail to meet this criteria and, in fairness, Stern Stewart do not suggest that any company should make them all. Any list of adjustments must represent a potential shopping list.

The final decision has to reflect practical as well as economic reality. To quote the financial director of a top 100 chemicals company: 'More than three adjustments and my general managers will tell me to forget it. They will go back to operating profit which at least they can understand.'

From a practical point of view technical perfection has to be sacrificed to be sure of achieving management understanding and commitment, as outlined in Figure 4.2. In reality this means that most companies will identify perhaps five or six of the most significant adjustments and limit themselves to these.

Figure 4.2
BALANCE BETWEEN SIMPLICITY AND TECHNICAL PERFECTION

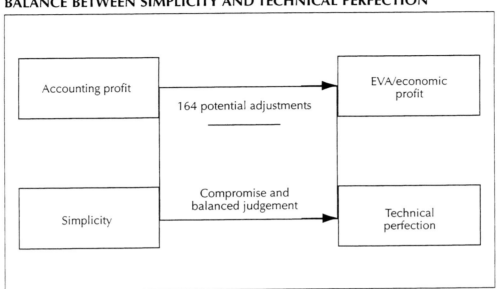

CALCULATION OF THE COST OF CAPITAL

Whatever adjustments are made, the component which differentiates EVA more than any other is the charge for cost of capital. We need to examine the derivation of this figure in more detail as it has a major impact on the EVA result. We said earlier that it is a weighted average based on the proportions of debt and equity agreed as part of the company's long-term financial strategy.

This is a topic on which whole books have been written and on which the experts only agree on one thing – that it is highly complex. The complexity mainly surrounds the establishment of the cost of equity finance. The cost of debt is relatively straightforward – it is the average interest rate on the company's loan finance, less the tax relief obtained by setting this cost against taxable profits. In the case of equity the cost cannot be seen in the same way. The cost is the rate of return which satisfies the needs of shareholders.

There are several different methods available to establish the cost of equity finance. The most common approach is the capital asset pricing model (CAPM) which was created by Sharpe, Lintner and Treynor in 1962. The model relies on the assumption that there is a linear relationship between the risk and expected return of any equity investment.

The model estimates a company's cost of equity by starting with the risk-free rate of return (i.e. the return on long-dated government bonds), adding a general market risk premium and then a further specific risk premium known as the beta. Betas measure the volatility of particular shares relative to the market and are published by a number of business schools – for example, London Business School and the University of Chicago – on a regular basis.

The overall framework of the model can be summarised as in Figure 4.3 which includes a few typical numbers to help understanding.

Figure 4.3
OVERALL FRAMEWORK OF THE CAPITAL ASSET PRICING MODEL

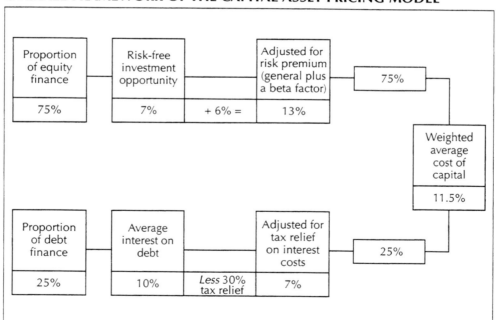

In this case the weighted average (75 per cent $\times$ 13, 25 per cent $\times$ 7) comes to exactly 11.5 per cent but it would be unrealistic to believe that any WACC can be accurate to the nearest 0.1 per cent because of the many assumptions built into the model. In practice one frequently sees published numbers to this spurious level of accuracy and it creates a false impression of their validity. Certainly the financial directors of top companies who see such numbers published externally along with EVA rankings frequently dispute their published number and the methodology.

One reason for the potential inaccuracy is that the model is based on long-term research of historical trends of the major stock markets. Therefore, in addition to many other assumptions, there is also the belief that the past is a good indicator of present and future trends. At one time the CAPM model was highly rated, with an almost mystical belief in its accuracy. More recent research by Fama and French in 1992 has thrown doubts on its validity – some would say to the point of discreditation – suggesting a potential tolerance of plus or minus 3 per cent. However, it still remains the mostly widely used measure of a company's cost of capital; it is easy to use and the basic concept of linking risk to return remains conceptually sound.

The choice of method is the subject of dispute between different management consulting firms. Stern Stewart, for example, favour the CAPM model whereas the Boston Consulting Group (BCG) advocate a method called the market derived discount rate. There are other approaches but these are the two which have greatest acceptance and are in most common use.

The market derived model approaches the issue from an investor's point of view. BCG tracks 100 of the largest companies and then obtains market predictions of their long-term free cash flow. This long-term cash flow is then related to the current value of these same businesses in the financial markets and a rate of return is calculated.

This method is an ingenious way of simplifying the issue. The argument is that today's market value is determined by the behaviour of buyers and sellers. This market value reflects the present value of expected future cash flows; therefore we can work out the return which shareholders require by projecting their future cash flow expectations and relating it to today's market price.

This approach has the advantage of looking forward rather than backward and shows surprising consistency of results over the years. It does, however, have two disadvantages: first, it does not attempt to arrive at specific company risk factors; second, it is only as good as the accuracy of the research into predicted future performance. Using the market derived discount rate method over the long term, the cost of capital of major UK companies in recent years has consistently come out as 6–7 per cent after tax in real terms. A factor for inflation would need to be added to compare with the rates in money terms which normally come out of the CAPM model.

Though these differences of methodology may be confusing and frustrating to those who are not closely involved, they should not be allowed to undermine the validity of the overall EVA concept. The critical benefit of EVA is that it encourages managers to be accountable for the assets which they utilise in their businesses. The point about the capital charge is not its mathematical perfection but its impact on management behaviour. Whether the charge is 9 per cent, 10 per cent or 9.3562 per cent the important thing is that managers understand that using assets must bear a cost. They will thus be motivated to manage their assets and cash flow more effectively.

A SUMMARY OF THE ARGUMENTS FOR EVA

We can therefore confirm the key strength of EVA. By including a line for cost of capital, EVA brings the balance sheet and the associated issues of cash and asset management – frequently given a low profile in financial reporting – into the profit and loss account, the main performance reporting document. Without this discipline, managers are inclined to focus purely on profit, ignoring the fact that there is a capital cost associated with its generation. EVA, in a single measure, combines all the essential elements of business performance and drives management behaviour in the right direction.

Another important benefit – though one which creates some problems of acceptance and comparison – is that EVA is a money measure rather than a percentage. It is an actual amount which management can be targeted to deliver after tax and after the cost of capital. It helps management to see that value is only created for shareholders when these costs have been covered and this message can completely change previous perceptions. Managers who thought they had a profitable business realise that they have been destroying value through a negative EVA. They will therefore be spurred into action, in particular to review the options for reducing the asset base.

The emphasis on money figures rather than percentages is likely to change behaviour in other ways which will be good for the business. There will be a far greater incentive to go for growth rather than maximising ROCE.

The following example demonstrates this point. A cost of capital of 10 per cent has been assumed.

	Company A	Company B
	£	£
Post-tax profit	30	100
Capital employed	100	500
ROCE	30%	20%
EVA		
Post-tax profit	30	100
Less Charge on capital employed	(10)	(50)
Economic value added	£20	£50

Company A with a ROCE of 30 per cent would appear to be very successful and management might not be motivated to seek ways to expand. In particular they might not want to become like B which only has a 20 per cent ROCE. If EVA is introduced, Company B is shown to be more successful, creating 2½ times more value, £50 EVA compared to £20. Therefore A is more motivated to invest in projects which may dilute ROCE yet which will still create shareholder value. Subject to risk assessment and normal project approval mechanisms, EVA should encourage management to invest in any project for which the return exceeds the cost of capital.

The following example further illustrates this point. An existing business is considering expansion.

	Existing business £	+	New business £	=	Combined business £
Post-tax profit	200		20		220
Capital employed	500		100		600
ROCE	**40%**		**20%**		**37%**
Charge on capital					
employed (10%)	(50)		(10)		(60)
EVA	**150**		**10**		**160**

If ROCE was used to assess the impact on performance, the opportunity would be rejected as it dilutes the company's ROCE from 40 per cent to 37 per cent. However, the EVA number shows that the new investment adds value to the business.

Conversely, when applied to a business with a low ROCE, the use of EVA may prove that new opportunities, though increasing ROCE, will actually destroy value.

	Existing business £	+	New business £	=	Combined business £
Post-tax profit	100		55		155
Capital employed	1400		600		2000
ROCE	**7%**		**9%**		**8%**
Charge on capital					
employed (10%)	(140)		(60)		(200)
EVA	**(40)**		**(5)**		**(45)**

In this example a company using ROCE would look favourably on the new business opportunity since the combined ROCE shows an improvement. The EVA approach shows that this decision would actually destroy shareholder value.

These two examples show that EVA is a measure which supports growth, but only if it is sufficiently profitable to create shareholder value.

One obvious implication of a negative EVA number is that, as the business appears to be destroying value, it should be closed down. This may well be the case and a negative EVA number will certainly encourage that question to be addressed, but it will not be as simple as that. First, there will be the strategic issues involved in such a major decision. Second, a more comprehensive evaluation of the financial implications would be necessary. This would involve the assessment of avoidable costs, the potential realisation of asset values and perhaps the options for selling all or part of the business. A full assessment of long-term cash flow implications and the strategic impact would be necessary before such a decision is made.

A final argument for EVA is that its use sends out a very powerful message to the financial community about the company's goals. By selecting a measure that links to shareholder value the company is stating that its primary objective is to provide the return that investors require. Perhaps EVA is now becoming so common that share prices will no longer rise on its announcement. On the other hand, failure to understand its benefits will create a negative impression to existing and potential shareholders.

ACTUAL VERSUS INCREMENTAL EVA

So far we have looked at the calculation of EVA and its benefits as a measure of performance. It is a performance measure which correlates closely to shareholder value and there is research to support this belief. Stern Stewart's analysis suggests a 50 per cent correlation, way above conventional accounting measures.

It is, however, *incremental EVA – the change from one period to another –* which has the closest correlation to shareholder value, not the absolute number. Thus top management should be setting targets of *improvement* to EVA and encouraging comparisons of *change* rather than absolute performance. This is a difficult message for managers to accept, particularly those who are performing well already and thus find improvement more difficult to achieve. The following example illustrates the point.

	Company A		Company B	
	This year	*Last year*	*This year*	*Last year*
EVA (£)	120	100	490	500

Company A only generated one-fifth of the EVA of Company B last year and just under a quarter this year. Yet when we assess *incremental EVA* Company A has performed more effectively: it has increased incremental EVA by £20, compared to B's reduction of £10. It is even possible for B's performance to be bettered by a business which has turned round from a negative EVA to a small positive number and thus created more value.

This message also has important implications for the balance between simplicity and technical perfection – for the decisions about how many of the 164 potential adjustments to EVA should be applied. If it is incremental EVA that is important then the debate about adjustments becomes less meaningful. As long as the adjustments are consistently applied year on year their impact on *incremental EVA* may well be minimal.

This point confirms a key message of this chapter. It is not the technical perfection of EVA that makes it such a powerful tool. It is its potential to influence behaviour in ways which are consistent with corporate goals.

5

Other approaches to measuring shareholder value at corporate level

> 'We're not interested in chasing growth or size for its own sake but in creating value for shareholders.'
>
> Brian Pitman, Chairman, Lloyds TSB Group PLC

Having looked at conventional profit measures and how they can be related more closely to shareholder value through conversion to EVA, we will now look at some of the other measures being used to assess corporate performance by shareholders and the analysts who advise them. In the past they were mainly concerned with earnings per share, the price earnings ratio and the dividend yield. Now new terms are being used and new concepts developed.

MARKET VALUE ADDED

Market value added (MVA) is a sister measure of EVA and is associated closely with it. While EVA is a shorter-term measure and can be used at business unit level, MVA takes a longer-term corporate view. It has received much public exposure from rankings of top companies which have been produced by Stern Stewart and published in the press along with EVA figures. As we mentioned in Chapter 3, MVA is really nothing new because it is similar in principle to the commonly used measure price to book ratio, except that it is expressed as a money surplus rather than as a multiple.

The actual formula for MVA is as follows:

Market capitalisation of shares *plus* Market value of debt

less

Shareholders' equity *plus* Debt on the balance sheet

As the difference between the market value and balance sheet value of a company's debt is not normally significant to the scale of the total numbers, the key drivers of MVA are market capitalisation and shareholders' equity. MVA represents the amount that the management have added to what has been invested and is therefore a reasonably good measure of value creation.

What makes MVA even more significant is its close relationship to EVA. It has been proved by distinguished accounting theorists and is generally accepted that the following equation applies:

Current MVA = Present value of future EVAs

The argument therefore goes that, if a business maximises its EVA, it will be creating value for its shareholders, assuming that MVA is a good measure of shareholder value. The problem is that MVA suffers from some of the same weaknesses as the more conventional accounting measures described in Chapter 3.

The reason for this problem is that MVA is just as dependent on the accounting conventions of each company as traditional measures. The market capitalisation number is derived from the market price and must therefore represent value for shareholders at that particular moment in time, but the shareholders' equity is derived from the accumulated accounting transactions of each company.

As with EVA, it is possible to adjust for some of the accounting vagaries, particularly those such as acquired goodwill which are likely to make a major difference. It can also be argued that, if you measure a company's shareholder value by the *change* in MVA rather than the absolute figure, most of these problems are reduced or more easily adjusted away. The fundamental problem remains, however: MVA is only as good as the accounting methods and the analyst's ability to adjust for them.

One other limitation of MVA is that it is difficult to use as a comparative measure. The result is expressed as a money value, either in total or in terms of growth from a previous period. This is fine for an assessment at a macro level; it is not, however, so helpful to shareholders who wish to compare the returns from investing a particular amount of money in a range of shares. Shareholders like to know what return they are getting, how this compares to other shares and how it relates to the cost of capital.

Though MVA is a helpful addition to the range of stock exchange measures which relate to market valuations, it is not a pure cash measure. It therefore does not measure shareholder value according to the definition in Chapter 1 – the combination of dividends and capital growth. It provides a better link to EVA than any other external measure and this clear link between the external and the internal is critically important. But we need to look further for the true measure of shareholder value as seen by those who really matter in all this – the shareholders.

THE BASIS OF SHARE PRICE VALUATION

We therefore need to revisit the equation of shareholder value as described in Chapter 1. This equation was based on cash generation rather than accounting principles and was made up of the following:

Price of shares when sold − Price of shares when bought + Dividends received = Shareholder value

Before we introduce the measure which relates directly to this equation – total shareholder return (TSR) – we need to think more about the basis of share price valuation.

Decisions by people and institutions to buy shares are based on their expectations of the future cash flows they will receive from holding that share and eventually from selling it. However intuitive, however judgemental, these decisions are therefore based on shareholders' forward projections of the above equation.

This principle is fundamental to understanding share price valuation. The forward projections will be based on perceptions of the company's future prospects and, where the share is publicly quoted, will reflect all available information. Thus the responsibilities of a management team who care about shareholder value must extend to managing future expectations as well as past and present performance. It also follows that value beyond the current moment in time can only be achieved by *beating* current expectations, an important point we will return to in the next chapter.

The current price of any share can therefore be expressed as a version of the above shareholder value equation:

Today's share price = Present value of expectations of future cash flows from dividends and from the price of an eventual sale

This can also be expressed graphically as in Figure 5.1.

Figure 5.1
THE TSR FRAMEWORK

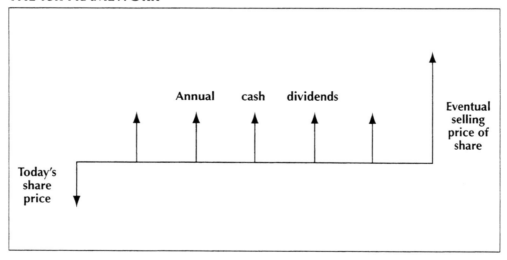

The date on which each particular share is bought and sold will vary by individual shareholder, but this does not invalidate the equation. Shareholders who are holding shares at today's price have the opportunity to sell at that price – their opportunity cost – and the

decision to hold on to that share is the equivalent of a decision to invest. Therefore the initial purchase decision in Figure 5.1 can be said to be made by all shareholders on every day they continue to hold shares.

The above equation also means that, whenever shareholders sell in the future, the price they receive will represent the present value of expected future cash flows at that time. Therefore Figure 5.1 could be expressed as cash flows going much further forward, even into infinity, and the date of sale would not affect their validity.

THE CONCEPT OF TOTAL SHAREHOLDER RETURN

All shareholders who buy shares have choices. They can choose to buy the shares of one company instead of another; they can sell one company's shares at any time and replace them with shares in another. Shareholders who are making these decisions need to have a means of converting the above equation and Figure 5.1 into a measure which they can use comparatively. They need answers to questions which are difficult to obtain from accounting measures and even from EVA and MVA analysis. Was that a good buy? What return did I make? Did I cover my cost of capital? Or perhaps more useful to the potential shareholder – based on my current projections of future dividend and capital growth, *will* that be a good buy? *Will* I make a good return which covers my cost of capital?

One way in which they make these comparisons is to express the equation as an annual percentage which is called total shareholder return or TSR.

This measure is not easy to calculate, particularly if the share has been held for several years. To explain this problem, we will look at some simple figures representing the holding of a share for a period of five years. We will assume that the shareholder is now looking back and evaluating the TSR retrospectively.

- Purchase price five years ago – £100.

- Dividends each year for five years – £10 per year.

- Sale price today – £150.

These figures can be converted into the diagram shown in Figure 5.2 using the earlier format.

Figure 5.2
HOLDING A SHARE FOR FIVE YEARS

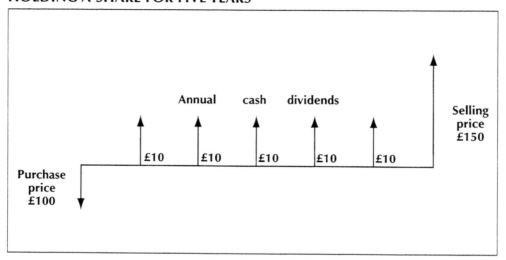

We now need to calculate the value which has been created for shareholders over that period and express it in a way which can be compared with other shares. The shareholder will also want to know whether the return exceeds the cost of the capital required to finance the initial £100. We will assume that this is 10 per cent.

The evaluation of this transaction presents a number of problems. At one level we could say that we have made a capital gain of £50 (£150 sale price less £100 purchase price) and received dividends of a further £50 but that would be a simplistic calculation. To calculate true shareholder value, we need to address some further fundamental questions:

- How do we take account of the time value of money, in particular the fact that the three key elements – purchase price, dividends and sale price – are all in different time periods?

- What assumption do we make about reinvestment of the dividends received during the period?

- If we make some kind of percentage return or present value calculation, how do we express it, and what do we relate it to?

Technology has made it possible to take information of this kind, put it into a computer program and come up with a percentage which represents the total shareholder return. For instance, any standard spreadsheet will quickly calculate that the TSR for the above transaction is about 17 per cent. For those who are familiar with the principles of present value and discounted cash flow, the method of arriving at this number will be familiar. It is the same methodology which arrives at an internal rate of return for the future cash flows of investment projects.

For those who would like to understand the full mechanics of the calculation, it is shown in the Appendix at the end of this book. For those who are only concerned with the meaning of the calculation, it is saying this:

- *Even if our cost of capital had been as high as 17 per cent, we would still have broken even on this share transaction.*

A further extension of the logic of this statement allows the shareholder to go on to say:

- *Therefore we must, on average, have made 17 per cent on this investment before the cost of capital is taken into account.*

It therefore also follows that:

- *If our cost of capital (the interest we are paying or the return we can get elsewhere) is 10 per cent, we have made an excess of 7 per cent over our cost of capital.*

These three statements are the basis of the power and flexibility of the TSR method of evaluation for shareholders. The questions they can then go on to ask are:

- *What TSR will this particular share achieve if we buy at today's price and the forecasts we are making about dividend and capital growth are achieved?*

- *What level of TSR has this company achieved in the past few years?*

- *How does this TSR compare with those of other companies?*

- *Does the excess over the cost of capital (in this case 7 per cent) compensate us for the particular risk we are taking by buying this share compared to other less risky (or risk-free) alternatives?*

More than anything else, however, TSR provides a practical means of comparison of the overall performance of all shares on the market. The results are highly dependent on the point of time at which the calculation is made (though this applies to any market-derived measure, including MVA) and care should be taken to choose a time which is not distorted by short-term market volatility. Also it is important that the results are seen in comparative terms over a long period – three to five years would be a typical timescale.

The power of TSR is that it helps shareholders to make choices. A potential investor is constantly faced with a range of options and need not go exclusively for one share rather than another. The thousand or million pounds available can be put into just one share or into a range of different shares. The investment can be in a million pounds worth of General Motors shares or a million pounds of Manchester United shares or half a million pounds of each. It is therefore essential to have a measure which can be used to assess share performance on a standardised basis and which compares the returns being made on all or any chosen group of shares.

This is precisely how Stock Exchange analysts use TSR. They produce lists of comparative TSR performance based on past dividends and share prices and they make their forecasts of future TSR before deciding which shares to buy and sell.

Figure 5.3 is a typical comparison made by the Boston Consulting Group of top shares in the consumer goods sector.

Figure 5.3
BCG COMPARISON OF TOP SHARES IN THE CONSUMER GOODS SECTOR

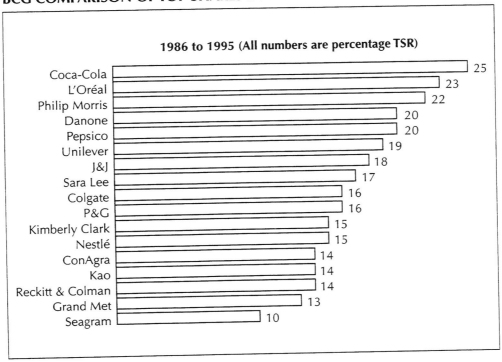

The popularity of TSR is particularly strong with the more powerful and sophisticated 'buyside' analysts, those who advise the fund managers who invest large sums in top companies. Many of the 'sellside' analysts – those who work for stockbrokers – still focus on earnings per share growth and the other conventional measures described in Chapter 3, perhaps because they are less likely to be held accountable for long-term return.

There are some purists who have concerns that this method of ranking may not always lead to the optimum return for shareholders, because their objective should be to maximise the present value of their portfolio. It is true that there can be occasions where a share with a lower TSR could create more present value than another share with a higher TSR. However, if one assumes the same level of investment and the same timescale for the comparison, this is a fairly unusual occurrence and does not invalidate the value and the power of TSR. In any case the important issue is that, whatever the technical imperfection of TSR, sophisticated shareholders like it and use it.

THE IMPLICATIONS FOR TOP MANAGEMENT OF PUBLICLY QUOTED COMPANIES

In October 1997, the joint chairmen of Unilever formally announced to the financial community that the company was no longer taking earnings per share and other accounting based measures as main indicators of its total company performance. They were to be replaced by TSR which became the single most important measure for the main board.

The statement to analysts said:

> 'TSR is the best single measure of the inherent value creation of a business. It needs to be measured over a sufficiently long time; we have chosen a three-year rolling period. As TSR performance can only be judged relative to other companies, we have selected a peer group of 20 FMCG companies, each international, each with sales of over $1bn.'

Unilever is not the first company to do this and will certainly not be the last; what was interesting and unusual was the public and positive way in which this change was announced. This reflects the increasing importance which major companies' top management and the financial community attach to having the right shareholder value measures in place.

Other companies regularly refer to TSR in their communications with shareholders. For instance, the following quote comes from the 1997 Annual Report of Heinz:

> 'The directors' commitment to Heinz Shareholders is reflected in the annualised total return of 21.8% over the past 20 years, compared to the average of 15.8% for the Standard and Poor's 500.'

One reason why the chairman of Heinz refers to the TSR measure is because he knows that his shareholders are also doing so. It is interesting to note the length of the period taken and the reference to relative performance against other top companies (Standard and Poor is a US agency which ranks companies' performance and credit rating and the '500' is their assessment of the 500 largest.) Though Heinz may like to quote a 20-year horizon, it is probable that stock exchange analysts would take a similar view to Unilever and look at a period of three or five years. They would also be more likely to compare with other shares in the consumer goods sector rather than with all top companies.

The logic behind the move to TSR by Unilever, Heinz and other top companies is unarguable. Their consultations with increasingly sophisticated shareholders, with the analysts who advise them and with the expert management consultants who are working in this area has led them to realise that TSR is the main and most valid measure which shareholders use to evaluate the relative performance of shares. As the top management of companies are employed by shareholders to create value for them, it is logical and essential that they should measure themselves by TSR too.

THE LINK BETWEEN TSR AND EVA

Unilever, in common with many other top companies, had already been using its own version of EVA for a number of years. This was seen as a first and important move towards establishing measures more closely related to value creation. However, EVA was seen as going no more than part of the way towards the full shareholder value measurement which TSR represents.

For Unilever EVA was a useful first step because it could be relatively easily derived from adjustments to accounting-based measures and could be used to measure the performance of business units within the overall company. However, the link between EVA and TSR is not as straightforward and as proven as the link to MVA. The next chapter will explore these links further. It will also examine how far it is possible to cascade an externally derived measure like TSR down to the decision-making processes of each business.

6

Cascading shareholder value measures into the business

> 'Our goal is to deliver value to investors in Quaker that meets or even goes beyond their initial expectations. Cash flow is critical to meeting this goal ...'
>
> W. D. Smithbury, Chairman and CEO, Quaker

If TSR is accepted as the measure of financial performance which best reflects shareholder value, the task of top management is to cascade this measure down to all business units, to ensure that the decisions of managers in each unit are thereby aligned to shareholder value. This can be achieved by converting the TSR framework described in Chapter 5 into an equivalent long-term cash flow for a business unit. The external TSR becomes an internal TSR, also often referred to as a TBR or total business return.

To quote again the statement made by Unilever to stock market analysts on the announcement of TSR as its main corporate financial objective:

> 'We have developed an internal measure which mirrors TSR but which can be used within Unilever. We call this total business return or TBR ... it will align the targets for management throughout Unilever with the corporate target and change the behaviour of our managers.'

In order to distinguish the internal from the external, we will from this point use the TBR acronym when referring to the internal application of TSR to business units. There are similar models with different names but the principles remain the same. A business unit is required to convert its long-term plan into a cash flow using TSR principles, in the same way as it might prepare a forecast cash flow for a major investment project. The cash flow is then converted to its present value and a total business return (i.e. internal rate of return) is calculated. The time period is a question of judgement, based on the company's business cycle and the features of the business sector.

This sounds easy in principle but in practice it is not easy at all. Yet it is a necessary process if TSR is to be cascaded down effectively. First, in Figure 6.1 we will revisit the TSR framework which was introduced in the previous chapter.

Figure 6.1
THE TSR FRAMEWORK

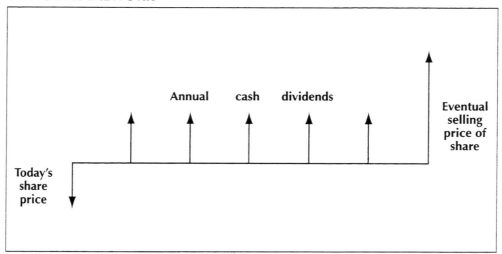

In theory the equivalent to this cash flow can be produced for any business unit, either as a retrospective analysis or a forward projection. All that is required are the equivalent cash flow components. The TBR model therefore looks like Figure 6.2.

Figure 6.2
THE TBR MODEL

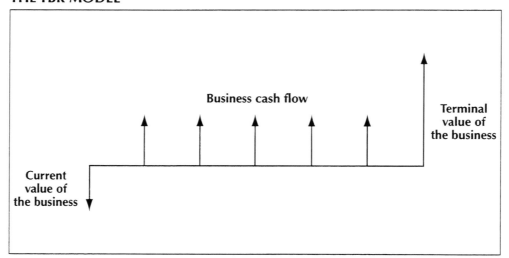

The cash flows generated from that business unit during the relevant time periods are the equivalent to annual cash dividends. The cash flow can be derived from profit with adjustments for non-cash items and asset changes – similar to the free cash flow as described in Chapter 3. Or it can be taken as the net surplus or deficit from bank account changes. It is the net amount of cash delivered to the centre by that business unit during that period.

The much more difficult problem is arriving at the equivalent of opening and closing share prices in TSR – the calculation of current and terminal values for each business unit. This is not easy and can get very complicated. There are a number of possible approaches, none perfect and all likely to be challenged.

THE CALCULATION OF CURRENT AND TERMINAL VALUES

For a publicly quoted company there is no need to arrive at a business value to calculate TSR because the share price is there every day. As mentioned in Chapter 3, it is normal to express this share price as a multiple of the latest annual earnings and to compare it with others, through the price earnings or P/E ratio.

The P/E ratio is also used by analysts and managers as a way of valuing businesses, particularly during takeover or business sale negotiations. 'This business is worth 20 times earnings because that's the average P/E multiple of similar businesses on the stock exchange' would be a typical negotiating stance. Thus it is possible to use a typical P/E multiple as a way of arriving at the opening and closing value for the TBR model.

This method is rather arbitrary and is dependent on the accounting methods used to calculate earnings. Other more sophisticated approaches to valuation have therefore been developed. Some analysts add back depreciation to earnings and work out a typical multiple on that number, though clearly a different, lower multiple would have to be taken. Other analysts recommend yet more sophisticated methods involving asset valuations, multiples of EVA, a factor for likely growth and complex formulae to reflect stock market assumptions. As we saw in Chapter 1, there can be highly complex equations to arrive at business values and too much complexity can detract from their usefulness.

There are reasons why technical perfection in this area is less important than is often thought. There is never a single answer to the valuation of a business, any more than there is a single answer to the valuation of a car or a house. Provided the same method is applied to both the current and terminal values, it is not necessary to become too concerned about perfection. The value is created by *changes* to the factors which drive value, not the absolute numbers themselves. It is likely that, however complex the model, the key factors within the control of operational managers and which drive long-term cash flow – what are known as *value drivers* – will be the same:

- profit margin improvement;

- volume growth;

- fixed asset and working capital control.

Value can only be created by managing these drivers more effectively and thereby generating future cash flow. There may be other non-operational factors which also drive value – such as taxation levels and the cost of capital – but the above three drivers are likely to be the most sensitive and the most controllable.

CREATING VALUE BY BEATING EXPECTATIONS

We mentioned in the last chapter that share prices reflect *expectations* about the future performance of a business. The TBR approach involves saying to the management of a business unit – we are giving you a business and assuming a value which mirrors the market capitalisation it would have if it was independent. This means that there are certain expectations built into this opening value. Further shareholder value can only be created by beating those expectations, either by generating more cash flow than is expected or by making the terminal value of the business worth more than it is now.

The valuation methods usually have the following expectations built in:

- profit margin to be held at present level;

- growth to be in line with the market;

- fixed assets and working capital to grow in proportion to sales.

Thus any improvement on the above will create value for shareholders and will feed through into TBR and into total company TSR. A complexity built into some companies' models is the assumption that, over the long term, share prices reflect an expected convergence towards average performance by both successful and unsuccessful companies. The valuations of successful companies, those making above average returns, assume that their performance will decline over time due to competitive forces. Thus a highly successful company, for example one making a high ROCE, will create value just by continuing its existing level of profitability and therefore beating expectations.

On the other hand these models also assume that the performance of unsuccessful companies, those making below average returns, will rise towards the market norm as they improve their competitive position. Thus value can only be created if performance improves at a higher rate than the assumption built into the model.

APPLYING THE TBR FRAMEWORK

Clearly this framework is only valid for long-term planning and analysis purposes. Like all cash flow measures and models, it does not provide an easy way of measuring performance in one particular year. What it does do very powerfully is to provide the framework for setting operational performance targets which feed through to generate cash and therefore shareholder value.

From a strategic plan based on TBR should flow targets in respect of the above value drivers – margin, growth, fixed asset spending and working capital control – all geared to the value-creating strategy of each business. The problem then is how to measure these on a day-to-day basis by a composite financial measure which reflects all these value drivers. There can of course be separate targets for each driver but it is also helpful for these to be crystallised into one measure – the 'big one' – through which the business unit top team can monitor their performance against plan.

The question therefore has to be asked: 'What single short-term measure incorporates growth, margin, fixed assets and working capital control in one number?' There is only one answer and that is our old friend EVA. EVA is the best link between shareholder value as measured by TBR, TSR or any similar measure because it reflects the same value drivers. And it does so in a way which is easily related to traditional accounting and existing reporting systems.

The link between TSR and EVA can therefore be seen as shown in Figure 6.3.

Figure 6.3
LINK BETWEEN TSR AND EVA

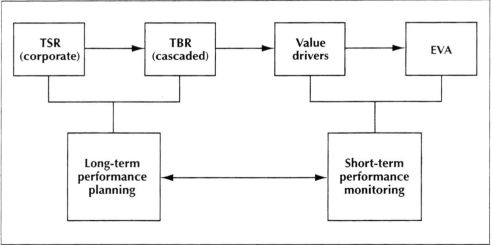

This relationship can best be summarised by a final quote from the Unilever statement (note that trading contribution is Unilever's version of EVA):

'Trading contribution, which is now established within Unilever, is the best short-term measure of value creation – it provides us with the best measure of progress towards our TSR objective.'

This does not mean that every business unit is asked to maximise EVA and that the best business is the one with the highest number. *It means that every business must have a unique EVA target which relates to its strategy and to its existing business situation.* We said in Chapter 4 that research indicates that it is the *incremental EVA,* i.e. its improvement from the previous period, which is related to shareholder value rather than the absolute number. Thus – and this is a very hard message to get over – the business turning around from negative to positive EVA by improving its value drivers may produce more shareholder value than an average performer which is not improving. The implications of using the TSR/TBR model is that value is only created by improvement from that point, by beating expectations.

Though the use of TBR is popular and links closely to TSR as used by major shareholders, it still has some of the disadvantages of any percentage measure – in particular it can discourage the maximisation of value in money terms. It should therefore be presented alongside the net present value (NPV) of the cash flows of each business, at the cost of capital. Use of NPV figures will be particularly important where there are resource constraints or where there is a need to evaluate the implications of a number of alternative strategies.

CASH FLOW RETURN ON INVESTMENT

TSR/TBR and MVA/EVA are not the only new measures which are being associated with shareholder value. There is one other measure which has been used by a number of top companies. This measure is *cash flow return on investment* (CFROI – pronounced 'seefroy' by some).

CFROI has some similarities to TBR but is rather more complicated. The problem is that its complexity makes it more difficult to apply because, as we argued in Chapter 1, management understanding is an essential ingredient for successful application.

CFROI relates the free cash flow being generated each year to the economic value of assets. It requires estimates of the current value of assets and therefore separates those which depreciate and those, like land, which do not. A long-term projection of future cash flow is then made, assuming continued free cash flow and estimated residual values of assets at the end of their life. This cash flow is then discounted and the internal rate of return of the cash flows becomes the CFROI.

The answer is technically the most valid calculation of the real return on investment being achieved on a company's asset base at a particular time. It is, however, of little use unless it is understood and this validity is hard to communicate. In practice companies usually do CFROI calculations of this kind behind the scenes, to assess the present level of achievement and agree the target required. The answers are then converted into measures which are more meaningful at the operating level.

FROM MEASUREMENT TO MANAGEMENT

The approaches described in the last three chapters should be seen as a new range of products which add variety to the existing stock of accounting and cash flow measures described in Chapters 2 and 3. They should not necessarily replace everything which has gone before – they should add to existing measures and ensure their alignment with shareholder value. The introduction of EVA does not have to mean abandoning the use of ROCE and EPS because analysis of the links between EVA and these two measures can be valuable. Managers like to refer to indicators which are familiar and, if they are to be phased out, it should be only be done after consultation and a period of parallel operation.

Several times during the last two chapters we have referred to Unilever as an example of a company which has made fundamental changes by the introduction of measures related more closely to shareholder value. To complete this chapter we now present Unilever as a more detailed case study of TBR implementation.

UNILEVER – A CASE STUDY OF TBR IMPLEMENTATION

Unilever has long been well known for the quality of its financial reporting systems, adopting advanced concepts well ahead of others and looking to change its methods in response to an ever changing environment. One of Unilever's strengths has been a clear separation between the requirements of conventional accounting and the information needed to manage a complex and diverse international business.

One feature which differentiates Unilever from most other companies who are implementing shareholder value is that it starts from the base of a system of economic rather than accounting-based performance measurement. Unilever uses the concept of current replacement cost for valuations of fixed assets and depreciation; there is also a charge on working capital to cover the impact of inflation, an essential need for a business operating in so many countries of the world. This means that managers joining Unilever have to get used to a different concept of profit, often showing substantially less than would be the case under historical cost methods.

Advised by The Boston Consulting Group (BCG), Unilever moved to trading contribution, its equivalent of EVA, in the mid-1990s. It became the main measure of financial performance for all business units. Previously there had been a portfolio of internal performance measures, including cash flow, return on capital and profit growth. At the corporate level the key measure was growth in earnings per share. Hans Eggerstedt, Unilever's Financial Director, comments:

'We became concerned about the alignment of our measures with long-term shareholder value. We also found that a portfolio of measures was difficult for both the businesses and the centre to apply in practice. There was too much emphasis on profit, not enough on cash flow and return on capital. We wanted one measure which gave a better balance between growth, profitability and cash generation.'

Trading contribution is effectively profit after tax and after a charge for the real-terms cost of capital on net operating assets. As it has the above adjustments for inflation on fixed assets and working capital, trading contribution is a good measure of economic profit.

The impact on management behaviour of its introduction was significant. Says Eggerstedt:

'There was much more interest in the management of capital efficiency in the businesses. The cost of buying and holding assets was brought into the heart of our reporting system. There was also a much more proactive approach to the management of tax. Specialists advise us on the final decisions in this area but operational management became more inclined to recognise this important cost in their decision processes.'

For Unilever the introduction of trading contribution was only the start of a planned evolution towards a complete and integrated shareholder value approach. It was becoming clear from research and from contact with the financial community that the main measure of external performance used by Unilever and most other top companies – earnings per share – was not as closely related to long-term shareholder value as had previously been believed.

A team was charged with reviewing the various approaches to measuring value creation. Trading contribution was a good measure for control of short-term operating performance but a link was needed to strategy and to the measures which shareholders used to assess their return. There also needed to be agreed principles of value creation which could be cascaded down throughout the company, linking the external to the internal and the short term to the long term.

After a period of debate and consultation within the company and with BCG, Unilever decided to make fundamental changes. In October 1997 the corporate financial objective was changed from earnings per share growth to total shareholder return, as described in Chapter 5. The corporate goal is to be in the top third among 20 peer group companies.

The high profile of the announcement was mentioned in Chapter 5. Eggerstedt says:

> 'We wanted the change to be clearly understood by everyone inside and outside the business. This is not merely a change in financial measurement, this is a fundamental change in the way we run the business to ensure that everyone's efforts are directed towards value creation.'

Unilever's top management is under no illusion that this change, on its own, is going to provide competitive advantage. Many of its peer group companies have adopted shareholder value measures and are instigating similar changes. Eggerstedt continues:

> 'It is in the way that we cascade it down throughout the business that competitive advantage can be gained, and we are committed to making this happen. To provide the link with our TSR goal, TBR will be adopted as the key measure of performance at the strategic level and the value drivers will be monitored closely to ensure that plans are achieved.'

Unilever's version of TBR follows the framework described earlier in this chapter. Business plans are converted into long-term cash flows (the period is generally taken as five years) and the NPV and TBR are calculated. To do this there has to be a model which calculates the

current and terminal values of each business and this has been agreed
after much research and debate within the organisation. Says Eggerstedt:

> 'We wanted a model which reflects the reality of business values, what
> our businesses would be worth if they were independent companies
> floated on the stock exchange. Then we can say to our managers, the
> current value reflects what your business is worth now and we will
> measure your success by how much value you create from this point, by
> the amount of cash you generate and by how much more your business
> will be worth in five years' time.'

The model of valuation has been tested on historical data and has
proved to relate closely to the stock market over the long term. In
other words, if all the separate Unilever businesses are valued
according to this methodology, the total correlates closely to the
company's market capitalisation.

The valuation model has a number of interesting and powerful
features. It takes each company's tangible assets as a base value, the
argument being that a business with zero trading contribution (EVA)
will be worth exactly its asset base. Value above that level depends on
the amount of profit and the model has a series of multiples which are
applied to annual trading contributions, depending on expected
market growth. The resulting number – effectively the amount of value
in intangible assets – is then added to the tangible asset values to
arrive at a total business value.

The model builds in an assumed convergence factor, known as 'the
fade'. It is based on the premise that the stock market assumes that
highly successful companies – as represented by return on capital
– will decline over time. Thus value can be created by sustaining
existing performance, by making the same high return over a long
period. Unilever calls this 'beating the fade'. Figure 6.4 represents the
potential to create value of those businesses with the ability to
maintain their sustainable competitive advantage.

Figure 6.4
UNILEVER: 'BEATING THE FADE'

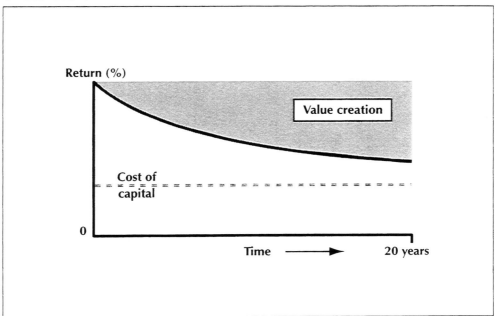

The implications of 'the fade' for strategic planning are quite fundamental. It is but one example of how the new value creation thinking will change expectations and encourage a totally different approach to target-setting. The highly successful business can create value by *sustaining* performance and beating 'the fade'; the less successful business will need to *improve* performance to create value. Sustaining and improving are becoming new words in the dialogue of strategic planning in Unilever. The balance between these two will vary from business to business, and is an important element of understanding value creation.

The *improvements* can come from a range of different strategies and a key benefit of TBR is its unifying nature. The balance between the four value drivers which have been identified – volume growth, margin improvement, working capital reduction and fixed asset control – will vary by company and different strategies will have different emphases. Says Eggerstedt:

'There have been two key benefits. First, businesses are able to test the value creation potential of a range of different strategies and there has been much greater insight into what creates value. For instance, growing a low profitability business will often destroy value – the emphasis has to be on getting the profitability right first. The second benefit is that the progress of businesses can be monitored against the value drivers which apply to them. You cannot run a major company like ours on averages, so we agree a TBR target based on the appropriate combination of value drivers for that business and we then expect them to deliver.'

The proven validity of the model means that, if every Unilever company delivers its TBR target, the corporate TSR goal should be achieved. This means that there is complete integration of internal and external measures. This is strengthened by the links from TBR to trading contribution which have been established. Eggerstedt continues:

'We see trading contribution as the final link in the chain, from strategy to operational delivery. Each trading contribution target reflects all the value drivers and is appropriate for day-to-day control of business operations. It is also now well understood in the businesses and our task is to make the link to TBR clear to everyone with value creation responsibilities.'

This involves an extensive communication process which will allow every key manager in the business to receive a concentrated programme of training. The framework shown in Figure 6.5 taken from a specially tailored computer-based training package is typical of the messages which are being communicated.

In addition to the computer package, there will be a series of seminars to reinforce the learning and it has been decided to train and empower the financial managers in every Unilever business to spread the value creation messages. Eggerstedt concludes:

'We want our financial people to be advocates and experts on value creation. It will be their responsibility to ensure that their colleagues understand and apply TBR. This is the way that value creation will be driven home into every Unilever business worldwide.'

Figure 6.5
FROM STRATEGY TO DELIVERY

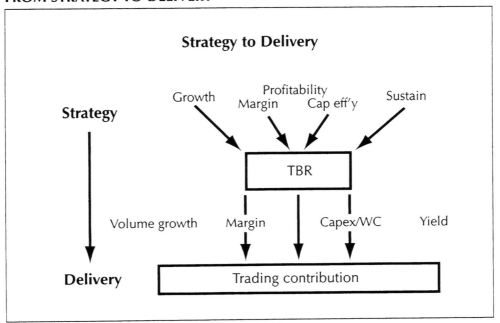

Unilever are moving quickly along the road to complete 'value-based management' and there are few examples of the necessary transformation being achieved in similarly complex international businesses. If Unilever can get there before the competition, the benefits will make a significant contribution to the TSR goal.

The next chapter examines in detail the nature of value-based management.

We would like to acknowledge with thanks the co-operation of Unilever and the Boston Consulting Group in the development of this case study, in particular for the reproduction of the two visual frameworks.

7

Value-based management

> 'I wrestle over how to improve value, from the time I get up in the morning to the time I go to bed – I even think about it when I'm shaving'.
>
> Robert Goizueta, CEO Coca-Cola (1981–98)

In the previous three chapters we discussed some of the new performance measures that are being adopted by businesses worldwide. However, as highlighted in Chapter 1, the setting of new targets does not on its own guarantee the desired result. Corporate measures must be translated into terms that can be understood and implemented at the operational level. If a company simply moves to new value-based metrics without cascading the right messages to that level, the chances of success are slim.

The word needs to be spread from the boardroom to the factory floor in a manner that is relevant and understandable to every decision maker in the company. The question is how? The answer is to do more than merely introduce new measures; the answer is to implement value-based management.

WHAT IS VALUE-BASED MANAGEMENT?

Value-based management (VBM) has been defined as 'a formal, systematic approach to managing companies to achieve the governing objective of maximising wealth and shareholder value over time' (McTaggart *et al.*, 1994). It represents a management philosophy which ensures that all decisions made throughout the company add long-term value. It is the way in which shareholder value is created and delivered at the grass-roots level. It is the way in which the whole company is energised in pursuit of value.

VBM is not a mutually exclusive alternative to other management theories. It can be implemented comfortably alongside existing management concepts and philosophies. It is a way of doing business, a way of thinking which must filter into the company culture and language to be effective.

VBM can be thought of as a three stage process:

- Stage 1 involves gaining an understanding of value creation in each business – what are the value drivers, where is value created and where is it destroyed?

- Stage 2 involves the design of a new set of key performance indicators which drive the necessary changes in management behaviour.

- Stage 3 – the final and essential stage which often gets too little attention – is a communication programme to ensure that all staff understand the importance of VBM to the success of the business and their own contribution to it.

STAGE 1: UNDERSTANDING VALUE CREATION

The key to shareholder value creation is to develop a strategy which generates future cash flow with positive present value that exceeds expectations. In companies which have fully implemented VBM, all management decisions are seen in these terms. Everyone in the company must have a rigorous understanding of how cash flow is generated by improvements to value drivers and how this arises from various management actions. Once the strategy has been agreed the targets for each driver must be cascaded down to the managers who exercise day-to-day control.

We said in the previous chapter that, in most companies, there are three key value drivers:

- profit margin;

- volume growth;

- control of working capital and fixed assets.

As well as identifying responsibility for control of all elements of these value drivers, top management also need to understand where, within the total business, value is created and destroyed. It is vital to know which segments are destroying value and therefore need urgent management attention, whatever their performance may have been under conventional accounting measurement.

The information gained from this value survey can then be summarised to provide an overview of how much value is created or destroyed by each business unit (*see* Figure 7.1). This will give top management some powerful insights and will often challenge previous assumptions about successful performance.

Figure 7.1
BUSINESS UNITS THAT CREATE AND DESTROY VALUE

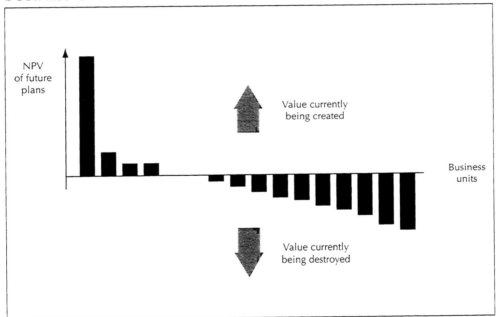

The above process is often called a value audit and provides a good starting point for the introduction of VBM. It can create some surprises and therefore needs handling carefully; managers who believed that their business units were profitable but now find that they are destroying value may not welcome the publication of a value map. They may also become opponents of the change to VBM.

STAGE 2: VALUE-BASED PERFORMANCE MEASURES

Tailoring the measures to each company's objectives

There is no perfect performance measure. Much will depend on the objective and the timescale. Percentage measures encourage a high return and are helpful for comparisons; value measures encourage growth and are helpful for target-setting. Short-term measures are appropriate for monitoring operating performance; long-term measures are appropriate for strategy development.

The key to successful implementation is to match each measure to its purpose and then to link them all together through VBM. The matrix shown in Figure 7.2 demonstrates how some of the new shareholder value measures we have described fit into the total picture.

Figure 7.2
MATRIX OF SHAREHOLDER VALUE MEASURES

	Short-term measure	Long-term measure
£ value measure	EVA	NPV (of future business cash flows)
% measure	Economic ROCE	TSR/TBR

There is no 'holy grail'; companies must select those measures which are most helpful to their managers and relevant to their business. The most appropriate measures should then be adapted to meet their own corporate objectives and integrated into the existing performance measurement system.

For example, as we saw in the case study in Chapter 6, Unilever have established trading contribution (a customised version of EVA which links to their own system of economic accounting) as their key short-term performance measure, alongside TBR, its long-term internal measure that mirrors TSR. They have also developed value drivers which provide the link between the short and long term, the long-term TBR target cascading down to determine the required level of short-term performance.

Quaker are often quoted as a company which has successfully made the transition to a VBM culture. Their tailored measure of short-term value creation is similar to EVA. It is called controllable earnings and is calculated for each division as operating profit less a capital usage charge. To quote William Smithburg, Chairman of Quaker Oats, who calls himself an EVA evangelist:

> 'We're not interested in how much income a division can bring in, we want to know how much capital it takes to generate that income. If the business can deliver discounted cash flows that exceed our cost of capital, then by definition we have created value for our shareholders. Our focus on controllable earnings requires managers to think and act like owners of a business.'

An article in *Fortune* magazine as long ago as September 1993 described how this worked for Quaker, how previous practices with regard to stockholding and factory utilisation were transformed by the new philosophy which Smithburg introduced. Steven Brunner, a factory manager at their Danville, Illinois, plant was quoted as saying: 'I used to treat inventories like they were free... Controllable earnings makes me act like an entrepreneur.' The article suggests a strong correlation between these changes and the 30 per cent increase in share price which took place around that time, though one wonders what happened to shareholder value analysis when the subsequent acquisition of Snapple was agreed!

British Airways has developed a special set of measures for their business. The basis for long-term target-setting is their tailored version of CFROI which is complex and would be inappropriate for communication to everyone in the business. To cascade this down they have therefore converted this measure to a simpler metric – their definition of operating cash flow as a percentage of the market value of net assets – and have set a corporate target of 17.3 per cent return. This measure is then converted to the appropriate value drivers – for example, passenger load factors, cost reduction targets, average seat prices – so that staff at all levels are able to see clearly the contribution that they can make to the company's success. The validity of a target with that degree of numerical precision could be questioned but what matters is that '17.3 per cent' is now part of the BA language and culture.

Cascading down the corporate and business unit measures

Shareholder measures must be adopted at corporate and business unit level but it may not be appropriate to measure all managers this way. For example, will all factory managers respond to EVA in the same way as Quaker's Steven Brunner? Will sales managers identify with and be motivated by this kind of performance measure? The answer is to know the people and the culture well enough to design measures which support shareholder value yet are also relevant to each group of staff. Some factory managers may be more motivated by targets based on meeting volume requirements, achieving input/output yields and reducing stock levels. The key is to understand the links of these measures to the value drivers and then set targets which are aligned to shareholder goals.

At Qantas key performance indicators (KPIs) were agreed through a 'self-discovery' process in which groups of managers examined the key areas of strategic decision making. These teams identified the nature of each major decision and the relative value to the business. The agreed set of KPIs was then incorporated into monthly reporting.

These KPIs highlighted the precise role of each part of Qantas in value creation. They also established accountability and an understanding of the interdependence of decisions. Most importantly they built an effective bridge between corporate strategy and operating decisions.

The hierarchy shown in Figure 7.3 demonstrates how, through this kind of process, strategy can be cascaded down the company to operational levels. At the top is the strategy and the broad goals which arise from it; at the bottom are familiar measures which can be used to assess the performance of operational managers.

Figure 7.3
FRAMEWORK FOR VALUE-BASED MANAGEMENT

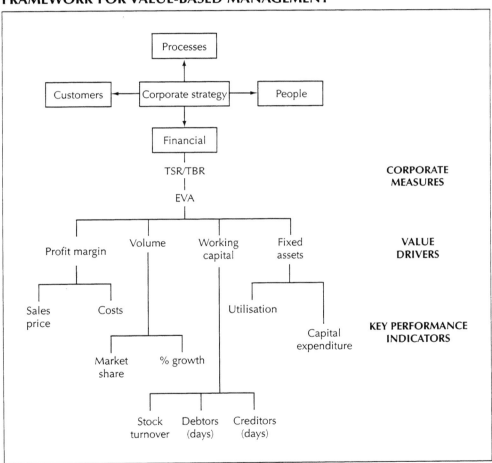

We also incorporate the need for non-financial measures through the balanced scorecard which we mentioned in Chapter 1 and to which we will now return.

Balancing financial and non-financial measures

The measures covered in this book have been primarily of a financial nature because that is its main focus. However, the concept of long-term shareholder value must go way beyond numbers. In a recent *Fortune* article Gary Hamel of the London Business School commented that efficient use of capital is not the only thing that determines successful performance. 'Strategy and innovation' he says, 'count for more.'

The balanced scorecard overcomes the limitations of a purely financial approach to the assessment of a company's performance. The precise selection of the portfolio of measures for each business must relate to its industry, its structure and its strategy. However, to demonstrate its practical application, the example provided in Figure 7.4 shows the set of measures used by a fast moving consumer goods company.

Figure 7.4
MEASURES USED IN THE 'BALANCED SCORECARD' FOR AN FMCG COMPANY

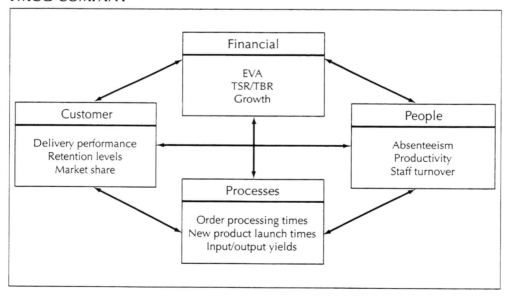

To be effective the balanced scorecard must be more than a framework which is produced at strategy meetings and shown in separate reports. It should be integrated into the planning and performance reporting systems, with non-financial measures getting their appropriate share of attention at top management meetings.

Linking performance to pay

In a recent article in the *Journal of Applied Finance and Investment* the Finance Director of Qantas, Gary Toomey, highlighted another important aspect of VBM – the benefits of employees sharing in the value they create for shareholders. This can be achieved by bonus schemes, share issues or other payment mechanisms.

On the subject of motivating people to act in different ways Toomey states:

> Of these, I believe the reward mechanisms are the most effective. Reward mechanisms need careful planning to prevent gaming or unintended consequences, but in several cases I have seen, they have been most effective in the realignment of attitudes and behaviours.'

Toomey's opinion is shared by management in many companies who have implemented VBM. The general view is that WYMIWYG – 'what you measure is what you get' – may be true but it is even more likely to happen if there is a financial incentive. WYMIWYG can be refined to WYRIWYG – 'what you reward is what you get'! In several major companies we were told that EVA and its equivalents only started to become embedded when the paypackets of top management were affected by it.

It is essential that, if incentive schemes are introduced, they are well thought through and encourage staff to behave in ways which create value for the business. For example, if a bonus is tied to ROCE – whether conventional or economic – the manager may be encouraged to hold back on investment unless there is a parallel growth target. This would not be the manager's fault – the WYMIWYG or WYRIWYG principle will drive behaviour.

At Fletcher Challenge, one of the largest companies in New Zealand, EVA forms the basis of their whole incentive scheme but, even so, they are aware of the dangers of 'short-termism'. To avoid this problem, the company operates a bonus bank system. Michael Andrews, the Chief Executive, describes the system as follows:

> 'Suppose a company declares a bonus of 100 for year one. The manager will be paid only one third of the bonus in year one. The rest will be paid into a bonus bank and will be released over the next few years, depending on continuing performance. In a lousy year, the manager will lose some from his bonus bank. It takes five or six years to clear the year-one bonus out of the bonus bank.'

STAGE 3: COMMUNICATION

A critical element in the introduction of shareholder value measures – the stage that will determine whether full VBM is achieved – is communication to staff at all levels. Some of the concepts are complex and, unless they are well communicated, the message will be lost.

People are only influenced and motivated by what they understand. When the new measures are introduced it is vital to have an organised programme of training for all those who are affected by it. The key is to make everyone in the operating units understand clearly how their actions and decisions contribute to value creation.

The communication of VBM requires careful planning. A common reason for failure is trying to do too much too soon. There should be a phased implementation as follows:

- **Top management.** This is the stage where much of the discussion and debate should occur. Top management need to decide on the key measures appropriate to their business and plan their communication process. The financial people should not be allowed to dominate here; all functions should have their say as it is the behavioural issues which are the key to successful implementation.

- **Senior operating management.** Once the key measures have been agreed at the top level, the debate should stop. The objective should then be to obtain buy-in from the management teams in divisions and business units by face-to-face meetings at which the new measures are explained. The key here is to show the logic of the new system – why and how it relates to shareholder value – and the benefits to all concerned. Once this support has been obtained, the measures can be introduced into central planning and budgeting systems.

- **Managers and staff throughout the organisation.** There should then be a carefully planned process of training, using all possible media to get the message across. This should go beyond written documents which are rarely as effective as top management assume. There should be the maximum possible time spent on seminars and workshops, with opportunities for questions and discussion about the implications. Depending on the size and spread of the audience, there may be a case for the development of a multimedia approach, involving video, computer-based training, seminars and written documentation. Converting everyone to VBM thinking requires the changing of mindsets and will not be achieved by one communication method or in one session. There needs to be a sustained and co-ordinated programme which is then integrated into existing training practices. Shareholder value must become embedded into the company language and the culture if long-term success is to be achieved.

It is difficult to generalise about the total timescale for successful implementation as it depends on many factors, particularly the nature of the business and the starting point of existing practice. However, from examples we have seen, it is realistic to think in terms of several years before shareholder value thinking is fully embedded into the culture of a large and complex company.

THE PITFALLS OF SHAREHOLDER VALUE

Articles in journals and business magazines tend to highlight the success stories of companies such as Coca-Cola and Quaker which have introduced shareholder value measures and ignore those companies where the benefits have not been delivered.

Commonly quoted reasons for failure are:

- **Performance measures that are too complex.** The search for technical perfection has often blurred the essential simplicity of the message and managers have continued to use the existing measures which they can understand more easily.

- **Lack of buy-in by staff.** This is usually because the communication phase has not been well planned. This is a particular danger when the management of the communication process is left to finance people. However expert they may be at developing the right measures, they may not see the learning problems that others have and may therefore fail to involve specialists to help them to communicate the message.

- **Using standard measures that are not relevant to the business.** The managers in some businesses, in their rush to adopt the latest new measures, have failed to take into account their financial structure and specific needs. The requirements of a service business – for example, an advertising agency – will be very different to those of a capital-intensive manufacturing business and measures like EVA will be much less appropriate. It is essential that the measures selected are relevant to the company's corporate objectives.

- **Treating VBM as a one-off project rather than an ongoing management philosophy.** Implementing VBM is not easy, it takes time and effort. Having been through the implementation process, top management may feel that they have completed their task. The opposite is true. VBM is about a permanent change in the mindset of all people within the business. It is only by constantly reinforcing the shareholder value theme and rewarding the right behaviours that success will be achieved.

THE BENEFITS OF SHAREHOLDER VALUE

This book has highlighted the potential benefits to be gained from moving to measures more closely related to shareholder value. In summary:

- **Change of management behaviour.** Value creation thinking becomes an integral part of day-to-day business life. The mindset of people within the business is changed from short-term profit to long-term cash flow generation.

- **A different view of profit.** Managers think beyond the conventional accounting definition of profit and regard the cost of capital as a key cost in their measurement of performance and in their decision making. They have a totally different view of how and where value is created and destroyed. Capital is diverted away from economically unprofitable areas in order to grow profitable businesses and products.

- **Consistency of measures.** Individual goals become clearly established and all lead to one corporate goal – the creation of long-term shareholder value. Managers become truly accountable and are rewarded for the right behaviours. They share in the value which they have created.

TWO CASE STUDIES – SUCCESS AND FAILURE

We will end this book with short case studies of two companies, one which got it wrong and one which got it right. The first company talked a good game but achieved little change in the behaviour of its managers. The second company has achieved true value-based management. The second company is the one that has consistently delivered value for its shareholders.

A case of lip service

This is an example of how it can go wrong. It involves a very large American company which announced the move to shareholder value measurement several years ago amid much public fanfare. The share price went up and the company became one of those quoted as having been transformed by the shareholder value approach.

EVA and the need for total shareholder return were mentioned in external communications at regular intervals. There was even confirmation that the balanced scorecard was in operation as the company developed measures of CVA and PVA (customer and people value added) to complement EVA.

The internal reality was very different. The messages did not seem to have gone down to the business units at all. People had heard of EVA, CVA and PVA in public pronouncements but did not know what they were and how they were measured.

For managers internally the key financial measure was EBIT (earnings before interest and tax) and there was no indication that tax or cost of capital should be taken into account. This was despite the fact that this is a highly capital-intensive business where asset utilisation and control of capital spending is critical. Earnings per share growth, ROS and ROCE were still better than competitors according to published figures. None of the company's managers could understand why the share price was so low. The answer was that shareholders had already worked out the long-term cash flow and were getting out while they could.

A new chief executive has now come in to turn things round. All his early statements indicate that he has found the opposite of a shareholder value approach in the business. This company talked the talk and may have meant it at the top level but did not cascade the messages down into the business. Thus there was no long-term impact from moving to shareholder value measures.

A case of value-based management

The best example of success we have seen is The Boots Company, a major UK retailer with interests also in the manufacture and marketing of health and personal care products. Boots were one of the first to institute the shareholder value approach, long before it became fashionable, and this may be the secret of their success. There has been a long learning curve and the concept has become truly embedded in the thinking of managers and in the language of everyone in the organisation.

The Boots Company use the term value-based management (VBM) and embrace the McTaggart *et al.* (1994) definition we used at the beginning of this chapter. Their internal communications stress that this is not a separate set of measures and concepts, it is an all embracing philosophy, it is 'the way we do business'.

What stands out in Boots is the way in which managers send a consistent message. When we have run management courses, we have been asked to integrate the VBM thinking into all our content. If ever we were to fail to make the right connection, someone in the company would remind us; it all comes down to value maximisation and long-term cash flow. This thinking is an integral part of the culture.

There has been a strong commitment to communicating the necessary messages in a way which everyone in the organisation can understand. Their 'VBM Manual' is full of helpful frameworks which show the link between shareholder value and the decisions made by employees on a day-to-day basis. The manual starts with the definition of shareholder value which we used in Chapters 1 and 5 – dividend and capital growth are stated up front as the only ways in which value is delivered to shareholders. Comparisons of The Boots Company's TSR with peer companies is openly disclosed and TSR is confirmed as the critical corporate measure. The manual reads: 'The best single measure of a company's performance is total return to shareholders relative to returns of similar or peer companies.' The manual also quotes numerous examples of other companies who have got it right – companies like Coca-Cola, McDonald's and Lloyds TSB.

There is an impressive openness about the way in which decisions have been and will be driven by shareholder value appraisal. The decision to sell their pharmaceuticals business is discussed in that context, as are decisions to open or close new stores. There is even public acceptance that, in hindsight, the acquisition of the retail businesses of Ward White was not successful because shareholder value principles were not properly applied.

In their application of VBM, the emphasis is on the appraisal of alternatives by assessing their value-creating potential – will it create value, will it destroy value, which option will create most value? They use their own planning model – similar in principle to the TBR approach described in Chapter 6 – to evaluate the present value of the cash flows relating to each option.

The most impressive thing of all, however, is the use of VBM as an integral part of the strategic planning process, with a strong emphasis on marketing analysis, on competition, on the need for sustainable advantage to create shareholder value. The overall framework used to communicate the VBM messages shown in Figure 7.5 is a clear indication of this.

Figure 7.5
BOOTS: OVERALL VBM FRAMEWORK

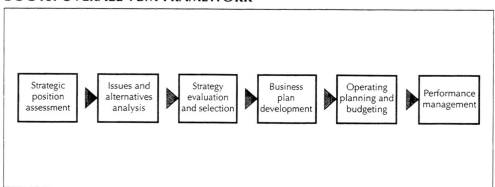

The final phase of the framework in Figure 7.5 – performance management – is the secret of The Boots Company's success in driving home the messages and converting them into action. The key requirements of integration and balance which we emphasised in Chapter 1 are clearly achieved. There is a strong emphasis on value drivers, with helpful frameworks to show the links to shareholder value. Figure 7.6 is a typical example: note the lack of mention of profit – just cash flow and shareholder value.

Figure 7.6
BOOTS: FRAMEWORK TO LINK VALUE DRIVERS TO SHAREHOLDER VALUE

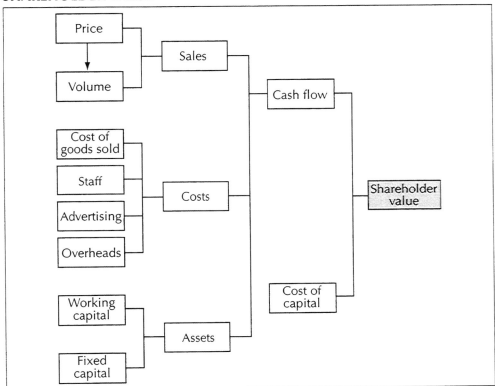

Boots do mention profit in their communications but it is always economic profit rather than conventional definitions. Managers are conditioned to think of the cost of capital as a fundamental part of the cost structure, not as an extra add-on at the end. Different divisions have different costs of capital to reflect their particular risk factors. ROCE is used but it is economic ROCE, always with a reminder that it must be combined with growth.

Their VBM communications also mention the need for a balanced
scorecard as part of an effective performance management system,
emphasising the importance of developing both financial and
non-financial measures which are aligned to strategic goals. These
should then be converted to KPIs – key performance indicators
– which are measurable and controllable. Again some helpful
frameworks are used to make this point, as shown in Figure 7.7.

Figure 7.7
**BOOTS: FRAMEWORK TO LINK VALUE DRIVERS, KPIs AND
PERFORMANCE TARGETS**

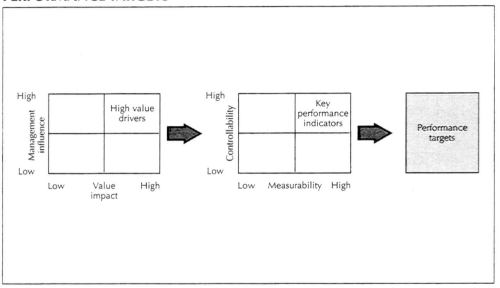

There is a clear statement that goals must be challenging and 'plan
driven' rather than unrealistic top-down impositions. The term
'performance contract' is used to describe the agreement of plans and
KPIs, stressing the need for commitment and motivation if results are
to be delivered.

In summary, The Boots Company has implemented value-based
management in a balanced and integrated way over a long period.
It has become embedded in their culture. It is the way they develop
strategy. It is the way they manage performance. It is the way they
do business.

We would like to thank The Boots Company for its co-operation in the production of this case study, in particular for the reproduction of written material and visual frameworks from their internal Value Based Management Manual.

APPENDIX

Arriving at TSR through the use of DCF techniques

We will explain the method by relating it to the share transaction discussed in Chapter 5: the purchase of a share for £100 five years ago, the receipt of dividends over the next five years and its sale now for £150.

We need first to convert the assessment of the value created by the above transaction from a retrospective to a forward-looking evaluation. We will assume that we are buying the share today for £100, expect to receive a £10 dividend for five years and then sell it for £150. If we do this, what return – what TSR – will we make?

Before we answer that question, we need to understand what is meant by present value and how it is calculated.

The concept of present value

If we compare the value of money in today's terms, there is no problem in assessing value creation. In the unlikely event that we bought a share for £100 and sold it for £150 on the same day, £50 value would clearly have been created. If, however, that £150 is realised in one year or five years' time, there has to be recognition that less value has been created. Money received in a year's time is worth less than money today.

The conversion of cash flows to present values enables us to quantify this fact but first we need to make an assumption about our cost of capital. The complexity of this issue has already been covered in Chapter 4 and we need not return to it here. For simplicity we will assume that the cost of capital for the shareholder is 10 per cent per year.

We can now ask the question – if £100 today is worth £100, what is £100 in one year's time worth? Or, putting the question another way, what would you accept today instead of the £100 in one year's time?

The answer – the *present value* of that £100 in a year's time – is £90.91 and the calculation to arrive at this number is 100/110. To confirm that this is correct we can assume that we have £90.91 now and invest it at 10 per cent; the answer would be:

£90.91 + 9.09 (10% of 90.91) = £100

Thus we have a means of converting money received in a year's time into its present value today. £100 received in a year's time is only worth £90.91 today, £1 received in a year's time is only worth £0.9091 today. Using this principle, we can apply a factor of 0.9091 to convert future cash flows to their present value.

In the above example of a share transaction, the £10 dividend received in a year's time is not worth £10 in present value terms, it is worth £9.091 (£10 × 0.9091).

This is known as the discounting process and can be continued into future years indefinitely, converting all future cash flows into their *present value*.

Assuming a cost of capital of 10 per cent the discount factors for the first five years will be:

Year 1	0.9091	(1.0000 × 100/110)
Year 2	0.8264	(0.9091 × 100/110)
Year 3	0.7513	(0.8264 × 100/110)
Year 4	0.6830	(0.7513 × 100/110)
Year 5	0.6209	(0.6830 × 100/110)

Returning to the shareholder decision, we now have a mechanism which enables us to quantify the extent to which the money-terms capital gain of £50 (purchase price £100, sale price £150) will be a capital gain in real terms. We do this by converting the £150 to be received in five years' time into its present value, to create a true comparison with the £100 being spent today. The present value is £150 × 0.6209 = £93.13 which means that this will be a loss rather than a gain in real terms. We must, however, make a complete evaluation of the transaction because the dividends received will compensate for this real-terms loss.

The full discounted cash flow (DCF) will look as follows (note that we are assuming that the sale was made just after the year 5 dividend was received; if not the sale price might have had to be shown in year 6):

Year 1	10 × 0.9091	=	9.091
Year 2	10 × 0.8264	=	8.264
Year 3	10 × 0.7513	=	7.513
Year 4	10 × 0.6830	=	6.830
Year 5	10 × 0.6209	=	6.209
Year 5	150 × 0.6209	=	93.13
Present value		=	£131.037

This can now be compared to the £100 being invested today and the shareholder is shown to be making a positive *net present value or NPV* of £31.037. To the shareholder, a positive NPV means that, if the cost of capital is 10 per cent and if the above assumptions about cash flows prove to be correct, *shareholder value will be created.*

Thus the concept of present value enables a shareholder looking forward to evaluate whether the purchase is likely to be worthwhile. If, however, the shareholder wants to go further and use this present value method to compare the share with others, this is still not easy. Other shares will have different prices, different quantities may be purchased and they may be bought and sold at different times. The above numbers must somehow be converted into a relative measure, which is the purpose of total shareholder return.

Total shareholder return or TSR is the application of a technique used by companies for many years in the context of investment decisions to shareholder value comparison. It is known by a number of labels in this context but most often as the *internal rate of return or IRR*. Other names are DCF rate of return and, perhaps the most useful description of its nature, the DCF breakeven rate.

Total shareholder return

The above evaluation of present value was based on the assumption that the cost of capital is 10 per cent. The net present value of £31.037 was entirely dependent on this assumption. A higher cost of capital (thus causing lower discount factors) would have created less present value. This can be demonstrated by taking another cost of capital assumption, let's say 20 per cent. The present value calculation of the dividends and selling price would then be as follows (note that the discount factors are now 100/120 cumulatively):

Year 1	10×0.8333	=	8.333
Year 2	10×0.6944	=	6.944
Year 3	10×0.5787	=	5.787
Year 4	10×0.4823	=	4.823
Year 5	10×0.4019	=	4.019
Year 5	150×0.4019	=	60.285
Present value		=	£90.191

If this is compared to the purchase price of £100, it can be seen that, if the cost of capital is 20 per cent, there is a negative net present value of −£9.809 (100 − 90.191). Shareholder value would be destroyed by that transaction and a shareholder with 20 per cent cost of capital would be unlikely to buy that share.

The internal rate of return (or in this context total shareholder return) is arrived at by trying different cost of capital rates and finally homing in on the one which brings the above cash flow exactly to £100 and therefore the net present value to zero. Already we can see approximately where that will be by interpolation between the two rates we have tried:

10% = NPV of   +£31.037

20% = NPV of   −£9.809

The rate between the two which crosses zero is clearly nearer 20 per cent than 10 per cent and we could do a mathematical or graphical interpolation between the two points to calculate this. However, the relationship is not linear and even the computer has to use trial and error to home in. If we try 17 per cent and 18 per cent we should have a better idea of where the IRR/TSR will fall. We will now introduce the £100 purchase price as a negative cash flow in year 0 – today – so that we can see the complete cash flow and the breakeven calculation more clearly.

Net present value at 17 per cent (factors therefore based on 100/117):

Year 0	-100×1.0000	=	-100.000
Year 1	$+10 \times 0.8547$	=	$+8.547$
Year 2	$+10 \times 0.7305$	=	$+7.305$
Year 3	$+10 \times 0.6244$	=	$+6.244$
Year 4	$+10 \times 0.5336$	=	$+5.336$
Year 5	$+10 \times 0.4561$	=	$+4.561$
Year 5	$+150 \times 0.4561$	=	$+68.415$
Net present value		=	$+£0.408$

Net present value at 18 per cent:

Year 0	-100×1.0000	=	-100.000
Year 1	$+10 \times .8475$	=	$+8.475$
Year 2	$+10 \times .7182$	=	$+7.182$
Year 3	$+10 \times .6086$	=	$+6.086$
Year 4	$+10 \times .5158$	=	$+5.158$
Year 5	$+10 \times .4371$	=	$+4.371$
Year 5	$+150 \times .4371$	=	$+65.565$
Net present value		=	$-£3.163$

Thus the TSR is nearer to 17 per cent than 18 per cent and can be expressed as 17 per cent to the nearest whole number. For forward projections this is close enough as the estimates are likely to be based on assumptions which cannot be quantified with perfect accuracy. If the evaluation is retrospective, looking back at what has happened over the last five years, further accuracy will be more appropriate and interpolation can establish exactly where the breakeven falls. Computer spreadsheets are programmed to calculate IRR/TSR to this degree of accuracy and will confirm the exact point of the TSR between 17 per cent and 18 per cent.

The meaning of TSR to the investor is explained in Chapter 5.

REFERENCES

Birchard, Bill, 'Making it count. How innovative companies really use the new metrics', CFO, October 1995.

Brearley, R. A. and Myers, S. C., *Principles of Corporate Finance*, McGraw-Hill 1996, p.180.

Fama, G. and French, K., 'The cross section of expected stock returns', *Journal of Finance*, Vol. 47, No. 2, 1992, pp.427–65.

'The real key to creating wealth', *Fortune*, September 1993.

Hamel, Gary, 'How killers count', *Fortune*, 23 June 1997.

McTaggart, J. M. *et al.*, *The Value Imperative*, New York: The Free Press, 1994.

Toomey, Gary, 'The role of value management in steering Qantas Airways', *Journal of Applied Finance and Investment*, Vol. 1, No. 2, May/June 1996.